T0147081

Anointed for
JUSTICE

ADRIAN LOPEZ

WESTBOW
PRESS®
A DIVISION OF THOMAS NELSON
& ZONDERVAN

Copyright © 2022 Adrian Lopez.

All rights reserved. No part of this book may be used or reproduced by any means, graphic, electronic, or mechanical, including photocopying, recording, taping or by any information storage retrieval system without the written permission of the author except in the case of brief quotations embodied in critical articles and reviews.

WestBow Press books may be ordered through booksellers or by contacting:

WestBow Press
A Division of Thomas Nelson & Zondervan
1663 Liberty Drive
Bloomington, IN 47403
www.westbowpress.com
844-714-3454

Because of the dynamic nature of the Internet, any web addresses or links contained in this book may have changed since publication and may no longer be valid. The views expressed in this work are solely those of the author and do not necessarily reflect the views of the publisher, and the publisher hereby disclaims any responsibility for them.

Any people depicted in stock imagery provided by Getty Images are models, and such images are being used for illustrative purposes only. Certain stock imagery © Getty Images.

Unless marked otherwise, all scripture quotations are taken from the King James Version.

Scripture quotations marked NKJV are taken from the New King James Version®. Copyright © 1982 by Thomas Nelson. Used by permission. All rights reserved.

Scripture quotations marked NIV are taken from The Holy Bible, New International Version®, NIV® Copyright © 1973, 1978, 1984, 2011 by Biblica, Inc.® Used by permission. All rights reserved worldwide.

ISBN: 978-1-6642-6602-5 (sc)
ISBN: 978-1-6642-6603-2 (hc)
ISBN: 978-1-6642-6601-8 (e)

Library of Congress Control Number: 2022908349

Print information available on the last page.

WestBow Press rev. date: 07/29/2022

CONTENTS

In those days *there was* no king in Israel: every man did *that which was* right in his own eyes. Judges 21:25

T he book of Judges took place at a point in time when there was no king in Israel. A time when the people of the land governed themselves and did what they saw fit. It was a time so relevant to our present day. Those days were parallel to the ones we live in.

Keep in mind, Israel is a nation that God chose for His own inheritance. It consists of God's chosen people. When the Bible makes mention of Israel it is also making mention of you because you are one of God's chosen people.

The king of Israel should be no one other than God Himself. The people in general, at that point in time, did not know their God. Therefore they had no guidance from Him. To have no relationship with the Lord is to have no king. To have no king is to have no hope.

When we read the words "no king in Israel" we can also get a clear understanding that there was literally no crowned ruler sitting on the throne. Nor was there a throne that one could sit on. This also goes to show that there was no real leadership in Israel.

After the death of Joshua, there was no longer anyone to

influence the people in the ways of the Lord. Without God and without any real leadership in the land, the people did what was right in their own eyes. What seemed right to the people of Israel, however, was evil in the sight of the Lord. The Bible says, "There is a way which seemeth right unto a man, but the end thereof are the ways of death" (Proverbs 14:12). There is a big difference between the way that seems right and the way that is right.

Jesus is the only right way. Scripture says, "Jesus is the truth, the way, and the life (John 14:16)." It is His teachings that we must learn to apply to our lives and His example that we must follow.

As we take our journey through the book of Judges we will find that the people of Israel were not living in accordance with God's will. They fell into idolatry, homosexuality, violence, discord, and many other sinful acts. We will be discussing their behavior as we proceed with the revelations that God gives us throughout our study.

As we study the book of Judges we will find a repetitive cycle where the Israelites do evil in the sight of the Lord, God hands them over to their enemies, they cry out, and the Lord raises a judge to deliver them from their oppression. When the judge dies the people go back to doing evil and the cycle repeats itself. The cycle is that of sin, bondage, repentance, and devotion, followed by sin, bondage, repentance and devotion. Time and time again this cycle repeats itself.

The cycle was repetitive in the times of the judges and it has also been repetitive throughout history. The word of God is alive and active or should we say, live and in effect. As it is written so shall it be. If it was a cycle then, than it will be a cycle now. The scriptures are still as relevant as ever in our present day.

Take a look around you and see for yourself. It isn't hard to recognize the turmoil and chaos going on in the world today. Idolatry, witchcraft, homosexuality, etc. Everything that took place during the time of the book of Judges is taking place at this very moment.

One of the most important pieces of information that we can get from this book is that God does not let sin go unpunished. Those that disregarded His laws were disciplined for their wrongdoing.

He disciplined Israel by using the hand of their enemies to dominate them. During the chastisement the people were pushed into a position to cry out and return to the Lord.

God is still actively using this same strategy today to bring His people back to Himself. This is why you see so many people living lives that have been dominated by the enemy. Overthrown by sex, drugs and alcohol. Stripped down to the bare minimum and suffering poverty because God has handed them over to their sinful desires.

This is God's way of getting our attention when we get out of line. It is when we hit rock bottom that we finally realize how much we need Him. He allows disaster to come our way so that we can cry out to Him.

The beauty of these scriptures is that God hears the cries of His people and does something about it. He raises up judges to deliver the people from the same oppression that He allowed to overthrow them in the first place.

The judges were imperfect people who God anointed to bring justice to His people. They had flaws and made many mistakes but in the process they carried out a noble task. They fought for the people and brought deliverance to them.

We all know that Christ alone is our Savoir. It is Christ alone who redeems us from sin and death and it is Christ alone that paid the ultimate sacrifice. Yet Christ in all His glory will use some of the least likely individuals to introduce Himself to the world. He does bring deliverance to His people by the hands of a chosen vessel.

Although there has always been a sense of the Lord's existence within our hearts, we never really got to know Him until a certain man or woman came into our lives to lead the way. The same way He used that man or woman of God to pray for you and fight for you on a spiritual level is the same way that He wants to use you to help others.

As we look at all the chaos and the ruckus in the world today, we can see how things are out of order. We can see the relevance of the scripture but we can also be optimistic knowing that God has a plan.

God always has a soldier to raise up. Perhaps that person is you. Perhaps He can use you for something greater than you have ever imagined.

There are so many lost sheep needing guidance in the world today and knowing this should make you want to rise up and be the leader you were called to be.

Perhaps you have heard the calling of God in your life but you didn't know how big of a deal it really is. You have been hand-picked by the Creator Himself. You are chosen to do so much more than you could possibly fathom. God wants to use you in such a way that He can be glorified through you. You were called to do great things. Very truly I tell you, whoever believes in me will do the works I have been doing, and they will do even greater things than these (John 14:11 NIV).

Maybe you're still in a place of struggle or maybe you are encountering a bit of suffering at the moment. These are things that we all have to go through. Maybe you're still fighting an addiction, or going through a divorce. Perhaps the storms of life have brought the tidal waves against your house and you wonder if it's possible for God to actually use you for something great. Continue to seek His face. He will heal you, and He will use you in ways that you could never imagine.

Getting involved in the work of God is to get involved in something bigger than yourself. If your heart is in the right place and you believe that God will use you to make a difference, then He will. As your faith is let it be done unto you. Find your purpose and allow the Spirit to guide your life. Do something for the King of kings and it will be remembered throughout eternity.

God is calling you to fulfil the purpose of an upward calling. In order to meet the challenge of this upward calling you will have to rise above your circumstances. Part of your calling is becoming an overcomer. If you can overcome your demons then you will influence others to do the same. God wants to use you to bring a great victory to His children.

As we continue our study in the book of Judges we will find that the people God chooses to do His work are the ones that are least likely to get the job done. He chooses men and women who most of us can relate to. These are flawed individuals who answer the call of God to bring justice and deliverance to Israel.

When we hear the word "judge," most of us picture a man or woman with black robes and a gavel sitting in a courtroom dealing with criminal cases. Although the judges in biblical times served a similar purpose in bringing justice, they were quite different from the judges we see today.

They were more like military leaders who fought to bring justice to God's people. Every judge that God raised up had the same problems as all the rest of Israel's lawbreakers. They struggled with the same sin and they were dominated by the same evil as everyone else. Therefore, it wouldn't make sense for any of these judges to pass judgment on the people. The Bible says, "judge not and ye shall not be judged" (Luke 6:37). Instead of criticizing or condemning the people from a position of assumed moral superiority, they fought for them. They rose out of the ashes of their own defeat to bring justice to those who suffered with them.

This is exactly what God has called you to do! He has called you to fight against the evil that has dominated your life and the lives of others for so long. In the process of overcoming you will become an inspiration to others who have struggled with the same sin you have.

There are people who refuse to listen to preachers who have not been in the same darkness they have endured. If you have not felt their pain then they might not want to hear you out. But if you have been in the same kind of darkness, and have encountered the same kind of evil then perhaps they will listen to you.

There is always a possibility of reaching people with no common background but sometimes it is a lot easier to reach an addict if you were addicted too. It would be a lot easier to reach an inmate when you have sat in the cell next to them for the last nine years. It would be a lot easier to reach the gang member if you have a history of gang violence as well. Sometimes this is just the way it works.

There is a reason for everything you have ever been through in your life. There is a reason for everything you are still going through as we speak. It is all a part of God's divine plan. There is so much power in your testimony alone. It gives hope to those who have been in the same darkness as you. It brings inspiration to those who are struggling with the same sin you once did. It brings light to those who live in dark places.

Your testimony is not limited to reach only those who have lived a similar lifestyle as you. Those people are just the most likely to relate. Your leadership will be influential regardless. God can use you to have a major impact on the world around you. He can bless you with influence. He can endow you with a spirit of inspiration.

And the children of Israel did evil in the sight of the Lord, and served Baalim: Judges 2:11

The children of Israel did evil by making a league with the inhabitants of the land and dedicating service to their false gods. They served Baalim which is plural for Baal. Baal was worshiped under many different names and attributes. This false god was known as Baalberith, Baalzebub, Baalzebul, Baal-Peor, Baal-Hadad, and Baal-Hammon. Therefore, the scriptures tell us they served Baalim or in some interpretations the Baals.

There were many images of this false god. In one particular image he was wearing a helmet with bullhorns to represent his so-called strength and power. He also held a spear that represented his control over nature. He was considered to be a deity associated with fertility, sex, pregnancy, childbirth, and crops.

In reality the Baals were nothing more than worthless Idols carved from stone. They had no strength nor power. They had no control over nature. They were unable to bring life or give life.

The people of Israel believed that the Baals had power and they served them. They offered sacrifices like sheep and bulls to Baalim.

They even sacrificed their first born children to this false god in times of crisis. This is a detestable thing in God's eyes.

It seems that we have arrived at the very same place today where people refuse to acknowledge that the attributes of deity belong to the God of the Bible. He is the only being who is omnipotent, omniscient, and omnipresent. He is sovereign. The giver and the taker of life. Infinite and eternal. Full of wisdom, power, holiness, justice, goodness, and truth. The God of the Bible is the one and only true God. We should always acknowledge Him as such.

> Prayer Call.
> Lord Jesus, we come before you this day to ask you for an accurate interpretation of the scriptures. We ask that you can be our teacher as we search your word for understanding. Enlighten us to the knowledge of your will. Show us how these very scriptures are relevant to our lives. In Jesus' mighty name we pray. Amen.
>
>

The second chapter of the book of Judges gives us a general idea of how the cycle goes. Sin, bondage, repentance, and devotion.

The first thing we have to understand about mankind is that we were created to worship. God created us to worship Him. Worship goes a lot farther than mere words. It is the dedication of one's life in service. Man will always worship something or someone because that is what man was created to do. Sadly, some have dedicated their lives to serve false gods like Baalim who were really no gods at all. They were merely statues or carved images.

Others, in like manner, have dedicated themselves to money, sex, drugs, fame, video games, and even their bellies. This is also known as idolatry.

Idolatry is the worship of something or someone other than God, as though it were God. It continues to be an issue with

God's children today. In these modern times, Idolatry has a way of concealing itself to where some may not even recognize it. Anything that a person prioritizes, loves, or values more than God is an idol. It could be a relationship, a job, an activity, an idea, or even a thing. In some cases people have fallen into idol worship by thinking too highly of themselves.

If we take so much time for the things that we are interested in we should also be taking time for Jesus. If we seek fulfillment, comfort, and satisfaction outside of God we are guilty of idolatry. We must learn to guard our hearts against the craving and the wanting. Understand that running to money, sex, and drugs, or anything else for that matter will bring about the chastening of the Lord. "If then you were raised with Christ, seek those things which are above, where Christ is, sitting at the right hand of God. Set your mind on things above, not on things of the earth" (Colossians 3:1-2.NKJV).

And they forsook the Lord God of their fathers, which brought them out of the land of Egypt, and followed other gods, of the gods of the people that were round about them, and bowed themselves unto them, and provoked the Lord to anger. And they forsook the Lord, and served Baal and Ashtaroth. Judges 2:12-13

The children of Israel departed from the covenant God. They turned their backs on Him and set their hearts after other gods. In doing so they were in violation of the first and second commandments: "I am the Lord thy God, which have brought thee out of the land of Egypt, out of the house of bondage. Thou shalt have no other gods before me. Thou shalt not make unto thee any graven image, or any likeness of anything that is in heaven above, or that is in the earth beneath, or that is in the water under the earth. Thou shalt not bow down thyself to them nor serve them" (Exodus 20 1-5).

They had completely forgotten all that the sovereign Lord had done for them when He brought them out of Egypt. They discarded the miracles He performed at the Red Sea. They pushed aside the memories of how He had brought their forefathers through the wilderness with an outstretched arm and how He led them to a land flowing with milk and honey.

The question is "have you forgotten all that God has done for you and all that He has brought you through? Have you pushed aside from your memory the miracles He has performed on your behalf and the victories that He has given you?" If so, now is the time for repentance for the kingdom of God is at hand.

And the anger of the Lord was hot against Israel, and he delivered them into the hands of spoilers that spoiled them, and he sold them into the hands of their enemies round about, so that they could not any longer stand before their enemies. Whithersoever they went out, the hand of the Lord was against them for evil, as the Lord had said, and as the Lord had sworn unto them: and they were greatly distressed. Judges2:14

Forgetting about God and replacing Him with someone or something else Is a good way to provoke Him to anger. He is a jealous God. With jealousy comes anger. This is why His anger was hot against Israel. He had the right to be heated. Everything He had ever done for them was credited to a carved image!

As a result He furiously handed them over into the hands of plunderers who took their goods by force. He delivered them into the hands of their enemies round about. They were no longer able to stand against those who rose up against them. This was done as a form of discipline.

We must also recognize God as a loving Father who chastises those He loves. A good father knows that discipline is necessary for a proper upbringing. For that reason He will not spare the rod. He will do whatever it takes bring you up in the way you should go. Even if it means giving you a good little spanking when you get out of line.

This kind of punishment would put Israel in a position to cry out. They would recognize the weakness of the false gods that they served and find that their idols could not fight for them nor save them. Then when all else fails they would come crawling back to the one true God.

Nevertheless the Lord raised up judges, which delivered them out of the hand of those that spoiled them. Judges 2:16

The judges were people who were called with a special calling to rise up and bring deliverance to their country. They were promoted by the Holy Spirit who bestowed them with remarkable courage and strength to accomplish their task. Each one would exercise influence over the people of Israel to guide them in the right direction.

We can always look at Israel as the church of God. When the people of the church enter into times of distress God will find someone to help. He will pick someone who is willing to contend for all those who are in a pitiful state. Perhaps God has placed it in your heart to pray, contend, and fight for the church today. If so, then this book has fallen into the right hands.

And when the Lord raised them up judges, then the Lord was with the judge, and delivered them out of the hand of their enemies all the days of the judge: for it repented the Lord because of their groaning's by reason of them that oppressed them and vexed them. And it came to pass, when the judge was dead, that they returned, and corrupted themselves more than their fathers, in following other gods to serve them, and to bow down unto them; they ceased not from their own doings, nor from their stubborn way. Judges 2:18-19

The scripture tells us that as long as the judge lived the Israelites were no longer in bondage, but when the judge died the people corrupted themselves once again. Therefore we get the understanding that the people were faithful to the Lord for as long as the judge lived. The judges that God raised up were effective in that time as they did what they were called to do.

They contended for their whole nation and made a difference. All across the world we are still learning from these judges today. This tells us that one person who answers the call of God can make a heroic difference in the lives of many others. It also tells us that the works of one person can be remembered for generations to come. To those that have ears let them hear.

Through this chapter alone we get a perfect view of the cycle and how it takes place. From disobedience, to discipline, and then it goes from repentance to deliverance. Keep in mind that they fall back into disobedience after the judge was gone. There always comes a generation who does not know their God.

Through this chapter we can see what happens when people walk away from God. The things which are anti God will creep in to overthrow.

Until repentance takes place there will be no deliverance. The Israelites have to face the consequences for their rebellion just like everyone else that decides to do wrong.

When we repent God will intervene and deliver us from our oppression. Through repentance, God is willing to bring us back into fellowship with Him. This is the most beautiful part of it all. The mercies of the sovereign Lord.

In Old Testament times God used flawed individuals to bring deliverance to His people. He raised up judges to fight and bring deliverance to those who were in oppression. The principle of deliverance flowed into the New Testament through a perfect person: Jesus Christ. We have a perfect Judge today. A Savior who delivered us without flaw. As His servants we are called to introduce Him to the rest of the world. When Jesus lives in you He will then raise you up and use you. He will work on you and through you at the same time. As this continues people will get healed from addiction and set free from bondage and poverty. If you truly are a willing vessel then God will use you. The extent to which He uses you will be up to your availability and obedience. Think big, believe big, and have an impact. As your faith is, let it also be done unto you.

3

Now these are the nations which the Lord left, to prove Israel by them, even as many of Israel as had not known all the wars of Canaan; Only that the generations of the children of Israel might know, to teach them war, at the least such as before knew nothing thereof; Judges 3:1-2

The nations that the Lord left within the land were the very same nations that He commanded Israel to drive out. It was because of their failure to do so that He left these nations in the land and used them to prove Israel. The word prove in this verse means train. These nations would serve the purpose of training the Israelites, by design, to become accustomed to war.

Many people at that time had no experience of war nor did they understand the concept of it. They did not know how to fight nor handle a weapon. Neither did they know how to drive out their enemies.

In the same way, there are people in this generation who do not understand the concept of spiritual war. They do not know how to pray nor use a Bible. Neither do they know how to resist temptation.

Nevertheless, the Lord will always find a way to stir up the warrior in His people. In those days, He used other nations to rise against Israel so that they would learn to fight.

In like manner, He uses the sin that we refuse to drive out of our own lives as a tool to push us into soldier status. It is amazing how God uses even our enemies to serve His purpose.

Namely, five lords of the Philistines, and all the Canaanites, and the Sidonians, and the Hivites that dwelt in mount Lebanon, from mount Baalhermon unto the entering in of Hamath. Judges 3:3

The pagan nations that were left within the land of promise were specifically listed. This brings clarity to whom the enemy was.

In the same way God will always give you the specifics to whom your enemies are. We all have an enemy list. We all have things that we know we should be resisting and casting out of our life.

Sometimes human beings have a tendency of considering other people to be the enemy but this is not so: "We no longer fight against flesh and blood" (Ephesians 6:12). Therefore at the reading of this list we have to think spiritually in order to identify our own enemies.

Although we may have been delivered from addictions, and diseases, God will always leave something with which we are to battle. There are certain things in your own life that God has not completely taken away from you just yet. Namely pride, gluttony, covetousness and lust. Well, maybe that wasn't hit right on the nose but you get the idea. You know who and what your enemies are. You know the areas where you still struggle.

And they were to prove Israel by them, to know whether they would hearken unto the commandments of the Lord, which he commanded their fathers by the hand of Moses. Judges 3:4

The word prove in this verse is translated as test. The Canaanites served two purposes. They were left to train Israel and they were also left with the purpose of testing Israel.

These nations were full of ungodly men whose practices were contrary to the word of God. The influences that they carried served the purpose of testing Israel's commitment to God. Israel was supposed to resist the sin, rebellion, and disobedience that was practiced among these nations.

Israel represents the church today, which has been placed in a wicked world with the commandment of not being conformed to its ways. We live in a world where wickedness is practiced all around but we are not to become involved with it. We are to resist the influences that come from ungodly spirits that move through worldly people. We are in this world but we are not of it. The influences and the temptations that you battle with each day are there to test your commitment to God. In the process you will know for yourself if you will remain obedient to Him.

The question is, "will you put up a fight against these temptations and influences continually until God removes them? Or will you succumb to the temptation and compromise until those things move in and defeat you?"

And the children of Israel dwelt among the Canaanites, Hittites, and Amorites, and Perizzites, and Hivites, and Jebusites: And they took their daughters to be their wives, and gave their daughters to their sons, and served their gods. And the children of Israel did evil in the sight of the Lord, and forgot the Lord their God, and served Baalim and the groves. Judges 3:5-7

The Israelites failed the test. They were told not make any type of league with the people of Canaan. They were also commanded to throw down the altars where these other nations worshipped their false gods (Judges 2:2). They did the exact opposite of what the Lord commanded. Instead of driving out the Canaanites they intermarried with them and eventually began to act like them. The influence of the lost people began to bring down the children of Israel.

It is important to know the dangers of getting involved with people who are under the influence of demonic forces. We are taught to love all people and treat them with kindness in hopes of reaching them so that they might be saved. Yet we must also be set apart.

By surrounding ourselves with ungodly people and intermarrying with them we have a high risk of picking up their behaviors. It is the things that they practice that we are at war with. Even Solomon (the wisest king who ever lived) fell into idol worship by intermarriage with worldly women.

When we encounter the people of this world we must learn to plant seeds and retreat. Let God use you to speak life unto the lost souls and then move on in the direction that the Spirit leads you. Love the sinner, hate the sin.

We must learn to completely eliminate the sin and temptation from our lives before we find ourselves becoming comfortable with it. If we allow sin to remain in our lives then it will eventually destroy us.

"Therefore the anger of the LORD was hot against Israel, and he sold them into the hand of Chushanrishathaim king of Mesopotamia: and the children of Israel served Chushanrishathaim eight years." Judges 3:8

The Lord was angry with Israel because they allowed the sin to remain in their lives. He was angry because of their disobedience.

The Israelites fell into idol worship and served Baalim and the groves. This was evil in God's sight. As a result of their disobedience the Lord delivered the Israelites into the hand of the king of Mesopotamia.

This means He handed them over to their sin. Any time we decide to put sin before God, He will hand us over to it and allow it to enslave us.

The king of Mesopotamia was an evil man by the name of Chushanrishathaim which means double wickedness. He ruled over Israel and afflicted them to the point where they became weary and cried out. When we choose to be sinful rather than obedient to God, He will allow the sin to dominate our lives to the point of misery.

And when the children of Israel cried unto the Lord, the Lord raised up a deliverer to the children of Israel, who delivered them, even Othniel the son of Kenaz, Caleb's younger brother. Judges 3:9

The first thing we read about this deliverer whom God raised up is that he was the son of Kenaz. Kenaz is Caleb's younger brother. This scripture is written in such a way that some are led to believe Othniel is Caleb's younger brother. This is not so. In chapter one of the book of Judges we will find that Othniel took Caleb's daughter to wife. If Othniel was Caleb's brother he would have been in marriage with his own niece which would have been considered incest. In the book of Leviticus chapter 18 verses 8-18 you will find that it touches on the subject of incest. You should not have sexual relations with parents, step parents, children, step children, grandparents, grandchildren, aunties, uncles, nieces, nephews, and even great nieces and nephews but it does not go as far as mentioning cousins. Othniel took his first cousin to be his wife which was not forbidden by the Bible.

In chapter one of the book of Judges we find that Caleb offered up his daughter in marriage to whomever would smite Kirjathsepher and take it. This means that the man willing to fight the Lord's battle would be worthy of taking his daughter's hand in marriage. Othniel was the man who rose up to the challenge to defeat the enemies of Caleb and Judah.

Caleb was a noble man who was known for his bravery. Out of the twelve spies who Moses sent out to the land of Canaan he was one of the two who brought back a good report. He was the one who silenced the people that spoke pessimistically about taking the land. He spoke courageously by saying, "We should go up and take possession of the land, for we can certainly do it" (Numbers 13:30).

He was rewarded for his bravery by entering the land of promise. His faith is legendary and still spoken of throughout the word today.

It would make sense to believe that the courage of Othniel was inspired by his uncle Caleb. We all have blood relatives that we would love to see converted into the extended family of Christ. This scripture tells us that becoming an inspiration to a blood relative is great possibility.

It is believed that Othniel was also from the tribe of Judah. The scripture tells us that Judah would be the first to fight against the Canaanites (Judges 1:1-2). This could be one of the reasons why the first judge would also come from Judah. Othniel had already smote Kirjathsepher and was already experienced in war by the time he was called to deliver Israel out of the hands of Chushanrishathaim king of Mesopotamia.

The Bible does not give too many details about the life of Othniel. We do not know the specifics about his flaws but just like everybody else that God has ever used, he had them. There was only one who has ever lived a perfect life and that is Jesus.

We do know that Othniel emerges in a time when God's people were living in disobedience. A time when they were under subjection to idol worship. He rises up in a time of compromise and rebellion.

These were the things that Othniel truly had to conquer in order to bring deliverance to God's people. He had to conquer the influences of the rebellious nations that were running rampantly throughout Israel.

With evil surrounding him on all sides along with the weakness of his own flesh it would have taken him a miracle to accomplish this task. It is a good thing we serve a God who specializes in miracles. We do know that Othniel had a wife from the tribe of Judah which means he was equally yoked with a good wife to back him up. This would make things a lot less difficult for him to accomplish his God given assignment.

The book of Judges was written in reference to the leaders that God raised up during the point in time when leadership was needed most. The Judges were God's way of dealing with the foreign domination that His people were undergoing. Therefore since the book is called Judges we will be focusing more on the Judges than on the darkness of the times.

And the Spirit of the Lord came upon him, and he judged Israel, and went out to war: and the Lord delivered Chushanrishathaim king of Mesopotamia into his hand; and his hand prevailed against Chushanrishathaim. And the land had rest forty years. And Othniel the son of Kenaz died. Judges 3:10-11

Othniel was filled with the Spirit of the Lord when he went out to war. It was the Spirit of power, of love, and self-discipline that motivated him to rise up and bring justice to the people.

The scripture does not give details on how Othniel fought this battle. Perhaps he raised up an army and marched out before them. It does tell us that the Lord delivered Chushanrishathaim king of Mesopotamia into Othniel's hand.

This means that the victory was from the Lord. Othniel's hand prevailed because the Lord was with him. If the odds are against you when God calls you to battle you must always remember that He is for you. God is the one who gives the victory. It does not matter what you are up against. If God is for you who shall be against you? When you are in accord with God's will and fighting His battles He will give you the victory and when He does your land will find peace.

It was because of God's divine intervention that the land had rest for 40 years. During the time of Othniel's life the people of Israel were reunited with their God through fellowship and service. Othniel was used by God to bring Israel back into communion with Him. Othniel was considered a hero in the eyes of Israel. What an honor that would be.

The stories we read in scripture about judges, kings, prophets, apostles, etc. are there to give us idea of what God wants to do with our own lives if we allow Him to do so.

Do you believe that God can use you to make a difference in the world today? As your faith is, let it be done unto you.

At this moment in time, God is still looking for men and women who would make themselves available to fight the good fight. It takes courage, it takes endurance, but it is definitely rewarding and worthwhile. Ask yourself these questions. Are you willing to let God use you? Have you made yourself available?

And the children of Israel did evil again in the sight of the Lord: and the Lord strengthened Eglon the king of Moab against Israel, because they had done evil in the sight of the Lord. Judges 3:12

After the death of Othniel, the children of Israel returned to their previous condition of life. The scripture tells us that they did evil again in the sight of the Lord. The evil they committed in this verse was in reference to the idolatry they engaged in, in Judges 2:11. The Israelites were stuck giving worship to a false god once again. They forgot all that the Lord had previously done for them. They turned their backs and walked away from the love and grace that He provided.

It was because of their behavior that the Lord strengthened the hands of their enemy against them. The Lord gave Eglon the power to triumph against Israel because He wanted to correct them.

In reality, Eglon had no power over God's people until the Lord appointed it. As God's children we have to understand that our enemies have no power against us unless God determines it. It is when we decide to step outside of His will that He determines to give our enemies strength over us.

And he gathered unto him the children of Ammon and Amalek, and went and smote Israel, and possessed the city of palm trees. Judges 3:13

The Ammonites and the Amalekites joined a confederacy with the Moabites and together they attacked and overthrew Israel. They were all common enemies against God's people.

These nations represent the evil that we are at war with in our own lives. When an evil spirit attacks and overthrows a person there is also an invitation for others to follow. That is why a person who falls short in one area without repentance is prone to fall short in other areas as well.

For instance, those who decide to participate in the usage of drugs usually end up becoming stuck in sexual immorality and other sins as well. Soon after compromising, the spirit of depression and hopelessness will move in to attack too. That is just the way it works.

The other nations that gathered with Eglon were close allies of Moab. Together they smote the city of palm trees and possessed it. This is exactly what evil spirits aim to do with those who compromise their faith. They would love to smite the children of God in order to knock us off of track. They seek to overthrow us and take possession of our lives.

The funny thing is that they don't even realize how God uses them as pawns to accomplish His own will on earth. God allowed the other nations to overthrow the Israelites but He did it out of love so that His children would no longer find comfort in sin. Keep in mind that evil spirits are influential to sin. When a person starts to enjoy sin, and seek it out, it becomes evil in God's eyes.

It is the very sin that one starts flirting with that the Lord will strengthen against him. What starts off as a little bit of fun will turn into a nightmare. The temporary gratification that comes from sin will eventually cause people to drift and before they know it, they become slaves to it.

So the children of Israel served Eglon the king of Moab eighteen years. But when the children of Israel cried unto the Lord, the Lord raised them up a deliverer, Ehud the son of Gera, a Benjamite, a man left-handed: and by him the children of Israel sent a present unto Eglon the king of Moab. Judges 3:14-15

It took the children of Israel eighteen years to realize that they needed help from the Most High. It took them eighteen years before they decided to cry out to God. Why on earth would they wait so long to cry out?

It could've been pride. It could've been shame. One thing for sure is that sin hardens the heart of humans. If we get caught up in it the deceiver will also do his best to make us feel too ashamed and unworthy to go back to God.

We must come to the realization that we can draw near to the Lord at any time. Do not wait till you are completely overthrown to come to the throne of grace because some people never get that opportunity.

If you are drifting away with your sin, rise up before you go too far. Do not let pride nor shame nor any other thing for that matter keep you from crying out to the Lord.

When things get ugly we would be insane not to cry out for help. God hears the cries of His people. As long as the heart is in the right place when we approach our God, He will hear us and help us.

God had a solution for Israel's problems. He chose to use an individual by the name of Ehud to rescue the nation from their bondage. Ehud had the same struggles as the rest of Israel. He had the same enemy as they did. He had to pay tribute to Eglon because he too was under subjection to him just like the rest of the people. God chose to use him despite the fact that he had spent years in bondage to the same evil and the same sin as everyone else. This is one reason why people say that God chooses the most unlikely people to accomplish the most unlikely tasks.

He sometimes uses people that might seem to others as unfit

for the job. The truth is that God uses those who make themselves available. If you make yourself available to pray, to serve, and to help others, then God will use you along the way.

There is nothing better than seeing God use you to make a difference in someone else's life. When divine activity flows through your life you will see miracles of healing and transformation.

Ehud was willing to make himself available. The Lord showed him that Israel needed some assistance and he decided to act upon it. He decided to be obedient rather than make excuses.

This man had every reason to make an excuse. In verse 15 it mentions that he was left-handed. In the Hebrew translation of this verse you will find that the words "hand restricted" appear in the text. This means that Ehud was restricted from using his right hand. It could be that he was without a right hand. It could mean that his right hand was injured or it could mean that he was born with some sort of deformity or physical deficit. Either way it would seem that Ehud would be an unlikely fit for the job. This is where God comes into the picture. It is in our weakness that the power of God is perfected. The good Lord specializes in bringing victory to the underdog. Ehud had every excuse not to fight back but he put his trust in God and made himself available.

The children of Israel sent a present to Eglon by the hand of Ehud. This was more than likely the tribute that they were forced to pay on a periodic basis. But Ehud had other plans in mind.

But Ehud made him a dagger which had two edges, of a cubit length; and he did gird it under his raiment upon his right thigh. Judges 3:16

The New International Version interprets the dagger as being a double edged sword. It was a cubit in length which is about 18 inches long. It was heavy duty. Long enough to penetrate deep into the human body. It was also double edged: "For the word of God is quick, and powerful, and sharper than any two-edged sword, piercing even to the dividing asunder of soul and spirit, and of the joints and marrow, and is a discerner of the thoughts and intents of the heart" (Hebrews 4:12).

The dagger that had two edges represents God's Word. There is always a scripture for every situation. There will always be a dagger for every enemy that rises against you. If you and your people are under subjection to any kind of sin, you can always search the scriptures for a dagger that is suitable for your situation. There is always something you can find to pull you out of the lion's den. Grab it, learn it, quote it, and cleave to it so that when the appointed time comes you can use it.

The Word of God is your weapon of offense. When you pray you should be praying it over your life.

It is no coincidence that your tongue is also shaped like a double edged sword. From your tongue the word of God comes forth and in it is the power of life and death.

If we were given the Word which is known as a weapon then you best believe we were given a battle. If we were given a battle then we must be prepared to fight: "Cursed is he who does the work of the LORD with slackness, and cursed is he who keeps back his sword from bloodshed" (Jeremiah 48:10 ESV).

If a man was sent out to war and decides not to use his weapon he most likely is going to get killed. If we want to survive spiritually we have to learn to use the word of God as a weapon.

And he brought the present unto Eglon king of Moab: and Eglon was a very fat man. Judges 3:17

Eglon was a very fat man and through revelation of the Holy Spirit we will find that he represents the spirit of overindulgence. This spirit brings an inordinate desire to consume more than one requires. This includes food and/or any type of luxuries as well.

Some people have a tendency to overindulge in eating while others go on senseless shopping sprees. Indulgence has a lot to do with one seeking pleasure in what they love or enjoy to the point of overdoing it.

Self-indulgence is also considered a form of Idolatry. There are some who place their own appetites above everything else. Instead of living to honor God they serve their bellies: "For many walk, of whom I have told you often, and now tell you even weeping, that they are the enemies of the cross of Christ: Whose end is destruction, whose God is their belly, and whose glory is in their shame, who mind earthly things"(Philippians 3:18-19).

Those who have chosen to dedicate themselves to their appetites for pleasure in the present time will find themselves miserable in the end. Instant gratification that comes from feeding the fleshly appetite is fleeting. True satisfaction comes when one dedicates themselves to the worship of God.

If you look up the name Eglon to find out what it means you will find the words heifer, chariot, and round. These were actually fitting ways to describe the character of Eglon who was a really fat man. It was probably really hard to get this guy off of the table.

Truthfully, everybody has a stomach and we all have to eat but we have to learn to balance and discipline our appetites. There is a difference between eating to live and living to eat.

We must be aware that the spirit of Eglon comes against us through consumption. The man was very fat and therefore we know that he symbolizes gluttonous behavior. He was an obese man. Obesity has many causes and could even come genetically but it is clear that compulsive overeating plays a major role.

When an eating disorder gets out of control it increases the risk of health problems. If one has a tendency to indulge in junk foods or greasy foods, then how can they expect to live long enough to experience all that the Lord has for them and wants to do through them. Our bodies are the temple of the living God. Therefore, we should be taking good care of what God has entrusted us with. The Lord will let you know what to be putting inside your body, the right amounts, and how often.

The Lord wants to preserve the health of His soldiers. The nature of our duty requires a healthy body. Eating properly is also a good way to recover from former habits.

Instead of minding earthly things we should be mindful of spiritual things which can be approached through discipline. We should all be anxious to learn the importance of balance and discipline. It is very important that we have a well-balanced diet. Not too much of just one thing. God created a variety for a reason. This is balance. On the other hand there are certain foods that you might want to exclude from your diet altogether.

This is where discipline comes into play. In the military, sweets are served in the chow hall but restricted from new recruits. This should also speak to us from a spiritual standpoint. There can also be a spirit of depression that moves through the consumption of fatty foods and/or sweets. This can also be a trigger that could lead a person back to drug use. This goes hand in hand with verse 13 (And he gathered unto him the children of Ammon and Amalek). When indulgence comes, it brings depression, and hopelessness and other demons to rise against you. The more a person indulges the more they strengthen their carnal desires.

As servants of the Lord we should be holding ourselves to a higher standard. We never want to let ourselves go. That is why we have to analyze our own lives to find what it is for which we truly hunger.

Do we have a hunger for God's word? Do we hunger and thirst for righteousness? Or do we spend more time feeding our flesh rather than our spirit? Whichever one we decide to feed more will be the most dominant force at work in our lives.

5

And when he had made an end to offer the present, he sent away the people that bare the present. But he himself turned again from the quarries that were by Gilgal, and said, I have a secret errand unto thee, O king: who said, Keep silence. And all that stood by him went out from him. Judges 3:18-19

After Ehud presented the tribute to Eglon he sent away those that helped him carry it. It was his own people that accompanied him to the king and helped him carry the tribute. Apparently there was a lot of money because it took multiple people to carry it.

The details of Eglon being so overweight also symbolizes greed. He was getting fat on Israel's money.

At this time the Lord had already revealed to Ehud what needed to be done. He would have to put an end to Eglon.

Those that accompanied him were of no help to accomplish the mission. Without the tribute-bearers there was easier access to the targeted man. If they tagged along there was a possibility of raising suspicion.

Keep in mind that they were still in subjection to Eglon and they may have been too fearful to get involved. Therefore, Ehud sent them away. As soon as they were at a safe distance he turned himself back from the quarries that were by Gilgal. Quarries are deep pits where stone and other materials are extracted. Other versions of the Bible translate quarries as idols. In the Hebrew text you will find that it is translated as stone images. Whether it was a deep pit, stone images, or idols, Ehud had to turn himself away from these things so that he could accomplish what the Lord had placed in his heart.

There comes a point in everyone's life when we have to make the same kind of decision. Either we can remain with the people who accompanied us in times of bondage and continue to pay tribute and dwell with the idols. Or we can turn away from these things so that we can be about our Father's business. We all have important missions to handle for God but it's up to each of us individually to be obedient to our calling.

Ehud knew that he still had some unfinished business to take care of and so he returned to Eglon. On his arrival he said, "I have a secret message for you, O king." Eglon responded with the words "keep silent" and sent all his soldiers out of the room.

And Ehud came unto him; and he was sitting in a summer parlour, which he had for himself alone. And Ehud said, I have a message from God unto thee. And he arose out of his seat. And Ehud put forth his left hand, and took the dagger from his right thigh, and thrust it into his belly: And the haft also went in after the blade; and the fat closed upon the blade, so that he could not draw the dagger out of his belly; and the dirt came out. Judges 3:20-22

Eglon was sitting in his summer parlor when Ehud returned with the secret message. It was small room built on the roof of his house, with open windows to catch the breeze.

Obviously nobody had seen Ehud as a potential threat because all the guards left the room at Eglon's command. They left with no objections. Perhaps it was because of Ehud's hand restriction that nobody expected him to play the role of a hero. Eglon felt comfortable enough to be alone with Ehud. While both men were alone in the room Ehud presented the message.

He grabbed the double edged sword that was strapped to his right thigh and plunged it deep into the king's belly. The dagger went so deep that the handle disappeared beneath the king's fat. He could no longer pull the dagger out so he left it in the king's belly and the dirt came out. This means that his feces and urine emptied. The message that was presented to Eglon was one of retribution. The message reveals the wrath of God upon His enemies. The spirit of overindulgence, gluttony, greed and everything else this fat man represents will be judged, along with those who put these things into practice.

The judgement of God will come upon His enemies and when it does He will not take it back. Perhaps that is why Ehud could no longer remove his dagger from the belly of Eglon. God will not take back His word. The double edged sword (God's Word) is full of warnings and promises that will stand for all eternity. One edge of this blade will be used to cut down all of God's enemies while the other will be used to cut away the sin from His children.

Concerning the spirit of gluttony, you will find that there are many in the church who have grown to accept it. Sometimes we can be our own worst enemies. There are people who struggle with the spirit of gluttony while others have surrendered to it.

To struggle is to put up a fight by wrestling against it. To surrender is to no longer put up any resistance. Those that still struggle with the gluttonous spirit must learn to use the Word of God as a weapon and declare it over their lives. Eventually the yoke of bondage will break but those that surrender to sin are in danger of God's wrath.

The truth is that we do not need any more gluttonous preachers behind the pulpit. We need warriors who can put the their appetite in check. People who have learned to maintain a balance within their lives. People who understand the importance of fasting and practicing self-control. People who understand what it means to show moderation and self-restraint. People who know how to put their bellies in check.

The spirit of Eglon attacks us through our appetites. That is why we must learn to put our stomach in check. Once we allow it to have dominion it will overthrow and enslave us.

It is the Spirit of God that leads us into all truth. He teaches us to use the Word as a weapon. He teaches us how to use scripture to fight.

Just like Ehud, we need a dagger to come against our own appetite. We need the right scripture to come against the spirit of indulgence. We need to search the Bible with our whole heart in order to find it.

It is true that there is a scripture for every situation we face. Those who are under subjection to the gluttonous spirit must learn to fight back with God's word. For example, remember the verse that Jesus quoted when He was being tempted in the wilderness: "It is written, Man shall not live by bread alone, but by every word that proceedeth out of the mouth of God." This was a scripture from the Old Testament that Jesus used to fight off temptation (Deuteronomy 8:3). When temptation arises we can follow the example of Jesus and use the word as a weapon. Ehud's dagger (double edge sword) represents the Word of God.

Then Ehud went forth through the porch, and shut the doors of the parlour upon him, and locked them. When he was gone out, his servants came; and when they saw that, behold, the doors of the parlour were locked, they said, Surely he covereth his feet in his summer chamber. And they tarried till they were ashamed: and, behold, he opened not the doors of the parlour; therefore they took a key, and opened them: and, behold, their lord was fallen down dead on the earth. And Ehud escaped while they tarried, and passed beyond the quarries, and escaped unto Seirath. Judges 3:23-26

After killing his enemy, Ehud still had to make it past the guards without raising alarm. From the sound of it, he casually went through the porch and locked the doors behind him. With a calm expression and a steady motion he made his way out.

Once he was out, the servants of Eglon came to the parlor door to reoccupy their positions of standing guard. When they saw that the doors of the parlor were locked, they thought that the king himself had locked them. They said to one another "surely he covers his feet in his summer chamber." This means they thought he was taking a nap.

They still had no suspicion of Ehud doing any harm. After waiting around for a while they became alarmed. They took a key and opened the door to find their king had fallen dead on the floor.

Meanwhile, this gave Ehud plenty of time to escape. God had specifically prepared Ehud for this mission and saw him through it. He provided a way out. This passage goes hand in hand with 1 Corinthians 10:13 (There hath no temptation taken you but such as is common to man: but God is faithful, who will not suffer you to be tempted above that ye are able; but will with the temptation also make a way to escape, that ye may be able to bear it).

Eglon represents the sin that is common to man. Although there is a temptation to sin, God will never allow it to be more than we could handle. With temptation He always provides an escape. Despite the fact that Ehud was surrounded by guards, and despite the fact that he had somewhat of a disadvantage, he was still able to escape. God provided a way out.

And it came to pass, when he was come, that he blew a trumpet in the mountain of Ephraim, and the children of Israel went down with him from the mount, and he before them. And he said unto them, Follow after me: for the Lord hath delivered your enemies the Moabites into your hand. And they went down after him, and took the fords of Jordan toward Moab, and suffered not a man to pass over. And they slew of Moab at that time about ten thousand men, all lusty, and all men of valour; and there escaped not a man. Judges 3:27-29

After the great escape Ehud made it back to Ephraim to blow a trumpet and summon the children of Israel. The sound of a trumpet is a call to battle. Ehud was calling God's people to take up arms so that they would regain possession of their lives, freedom, and their land.

A great many gathered together to follow him. It was more than just his great courage, and his victory over Eglon that motivated these people to follow him. It had a lot to do with his commitment, his integrity, and his humility.

It is the right character traits that will influence others to follow. These things can be developed in every believer who is fully surrendered to the will of God. Great leadership does not come from status, titles, nor positions. It comes from the quality of your character. When you allow God to develop your character traits you will also become influential with others.

God wants to invest in you. He wants to build you up to lead a people. He wants to see you through your struggles so that you may become more than a conqueror. Others will see your victories wrought by God and be encouraged to follow you.

Just like any other great leader, Ehud was able to communicate with his team effectively. He assured them that the Lord had delivered their enemies into their hand. Therefore they followed him and took the fords of Jordan towards Moab so that the Moabites could not escape nor get help.

They slew at that time about ten thousand men, all lusty and all men of valor. The word lusty also refers to fat. It means that some of these men were fat or rich from the plentiful land that they had put under subjection.

They had accumulated wealth from the Israelites and waxed fat from it. All that were lusty were slain and all that were strong were also slain. All those whom Eglon placed in this land to rule over them were slain. This is the kind of influence that one man can have over an entire nation.

Ehud's victory over Eglon motivated others to move in unison.

When one man allows the work of God to be done in their lives they will see victory, not only for themselves but also for many others. It becomes a chain reaction.

Likewise, this book comes with the sound of a trumpet. And also with the confirmation that the Lord has delivered your enemies into your hands. Rise up and become the men and women God has called you to be.

Despite his limitations, his weaknesses, and his flaws, God used Ehud. It was because of his obedience that Ehud was used so mightily. He was willing to step it up and become all that he could be. He moved in the strength of God and in the power of His might and many people followed after him. The Moabites fell before the children of Israel that day and the land had rest for 80 years. This is comparable to two generations.

And the Lord sold them into the hand of Jabin king of Canaan, that reigned in Hazor; the captain of whose host was Sisera, which dwelt in Harosheth of the Gentiles. Judges 4:2

After the death of Ehud, the children of Israel did evil again in the sight of the Lord and this time the Lord hands them over to Jabin king of Canaan. The name Jabin was only a title that was given to the kings of Hazor just like Pharaoh was a title given to the kings of Egypt. In the book of Joshua the name Jabin was also listed amongst the enemies of Israel.

We won't be reading much about Jabin in this book because the Bible mainly focuses on his commanding officer Sisera. This man was stationed in Harosheth. He had nine hundred iron chariots and oppressed the children of Israel with cruelty for 20 years. The harsh treatment that came from this man drove Israel to cry out to the Lord for help.

And the children of Israel cried unto the Lord: for he had nine hundred chariots of iron; and twenty years he mightily oppressed the children of Israel. And Deborah, a prophetess, the wife of Lapidoth, she judged Israel at that time. And she dwelt under the palm tree of Deborah between Ramah and Bethel in mount Ephraim: and the children of Israel came up to her for judgment. Judges 4:3-5

At the time when Israel cried out to the Lord, there was a prophetess by the name of Deborah who judged Israel. The Bible mentions her as the wife of Lapidoth. This is because Lapidoth was the head of her household and she honored him as such. Deborah had the gift of prophecy and she was also anointed as Judge. She had a ministry and a platform, yet she lived her life in submission to her husband.

This is something that a lot of females struggle with but when a woman lives in submission to her husband she is choosing to bless and be a blessing to him. As she complies with God's design for marriage she will then experience the fullness of joy that comes with it. By submitting to the leadership of her husband she is also demonstrating respect towards him.

On the other hand we can see the love that Lapidoth demonstrated toward Deborah because she was flourishing under his leadership. This usually happens when a man nurtures, and compliments his wife in all she does. It is important for husbands to invest in their wives and care for them enough to see them thrive in their own calling. That is exactly the kind of support Lappidoth was giving his wife.

Deborah dwelt under a palm tree that had her own name on it. She dwelt under the palm tree of Deborah between Ramah and Bethel in Mount Ephraim. This means that she found her spot in life and began to function and thrive in it. She was becoming the woman that God had intended her to be. She was growing and maturing in wisdom. She was utilizing and developing her God given gifts.

All women and men need to get to the point where we can do the same. We need to find our own place in life so that we can flourish in it. We need to dwell under the palm tree that has our own name on it. We don't have to act like anybody else nor want what anyone else has. God has a purpose and a plan for each of us individually.

In Psalm 92:12 the flourishing of a person is compared to a palm tree. Therefore we know that the palm of Deborah was the place where she flourished. It was a place where she found purpose. A place where she began to maximize her potential. A place where she truly embraced her calling to be a woman of God.

The children of Israel came up to her for judgment. They came to her to with all their problems and she counseled them. This was part of her ministry. As Judge she would settle disputes amongst the people. She would help them, encourage them, and give them guidance. She spoke in such a way that people wanted listen to her and she listened in such a way that people wanted to speak to her.

It is possible that many people came to her with complaints about the man Sisera who oppressed them with cruelty. Perhaps this is why she summoned Barak in the very next verse.

And she sent and called Barak the son of Abinoam out of Kedeshnaphtali, and said unto him, Hath not the Lord God of Israel commanded, saying, Go and draw toward mount Tabor, and take with thee ten thousand men of the children of Naphtali and of the children of Zebulun And I will draw unto thee to the river Kishon Sisera, the captain of Jabin's army, with his chariots and his multitude; and I will deliver him into thine hand. Judges 4:6-7

Barak, a chosen vessel of God, was summoned out of Kedeshnaphtali by Deborah. Destined to play a role in the deliverance of Israel, he came forth to hear the words of the prophetess.

She started by telling him what the Lord had commanded him to do. She told him to gather ten thousand men from Naptali and Zebulan and March to Mount Tabor. Then the Lord would draw out the enemy to meet him by the river Kishon with his chariots and his troops.

There was a promise of victory that followed these instructions. God said He would deliver the enemy into Barak's hand. The instructions needed to be followed in order for the victory to come to pass.

When we are obedient to the instructions of God we shall receive the promises of God as well. There is always a set of instructions to follow before we can ever receive the promise or gain the victory.

Deborah and Barak were two different people that God intended to use for the same mission. Deborah was the mouthpiece of God and Barak would be the hand of God in the battle. Two different functions yet they were part of the same body: "For just as each of us has one body with many members, and these members do not all have the same function, so in Christ we, though many, form one body, and each member belongs to all the others. We have different gifts, according to the grace given to each of us. If your gift is prophesying, then prophesy in accordance with your faith" (Rom 12:4-6 NIV).

Prophecy is a gift of the Holy Spirit. A prophetic word is a foretelling, a prediction, or a declaration of upcoming events. The only way that a person can utter a true prophecy is if it was given by God alone. He is the only one who knows the future. He is the only one who knows the end from the beginning.

If your gift is prophesying, then prophesy in accordance with your faith. Faith comes by hearing and hearing by the word of God. Therefore, prophecy comes by the hearing of God's word.

In Old Testament times prophecy was brought forth by a chosen vessel who was filled with the Spirit of God. God would speak His word to this vessel and then they would share it with others. God would speak to and through His chosen vessel. The prophecies included warnings and encouragement.

In New Testament times the Holy Spirit has been manifested and poured forth unto all flesh giving many more people access to the gifts. Just as God spoke openly to His children then, He will also speak openly to His children now. To prophesy is to interpret and declare God's perfect will and to make known His purposes to His people.

New Testament prophecy does not contradict the old. As a matter of fact it is rooted and grounded in it. God will never give a prophecy that contradicts what He has already said.

Even now we prophesy in accordance to the word of God. We prophesy by faith. Faith comes by hearing and hearing by the word of God. Prophecy also includes the ability to inspire, encourage, and comfort God's people: "But the one who prophesies speaks to people for their strengthening, encouraging and comfort" (1 Corinthians 14:3 NIV)

Deborah was an inspirational leader. She had the power to influence and motivate people to the point where attitudes and beliefs would be transformed. The quality of her character played a major role in the leadership she displayed.

The prophetic word that Deborah spoke to Barak was that Sisera would be delivered into his hand at the river of Kishon. This word was given by God Himself.

Here is a prophetic word for the reader of this book. If you will be encouraged to fight that thing which you have been struggling with, then you too shall see victory. God will deliver it into your hands. There will also be a group of people that will follow you into victory. These words are rooted and grounded in the Word of God and confirmed by the book of Judges.

Sometimes a prophetic word must first be received in the spiritual before it can ever be received in the physical. In other words, you will have to believe it before it will ever come to pass. If you do not believe, then it the prophecy is not meant for you. But there will be many who pick this book up and receive this prophecy over their lives and rise to be more than conquerors.

Usually when we receive a prophetic word it contradicts our reality because what we are hearing from God and what we are experiencing are two different things. That is why we walk by faith and not by sight. Faith comes by hearing. We hear God's word and we accept it as the truth despite what the situation looks like.

When Deborah spoke this prophetic word of victory to Barak he didn't completely receive it as the truth because of what he was experiencing at the time. He was lacking in courage and in faith. He refused to go to battle without the inspirational presence of Deborah coming alongside of him.

And Barak said unto her, If thou wilt go with me, then I will go: but if thou wilt not go with me, then I will not go. And she said, I will surely go with thee: notwithstanding the journey that thou takest shall not be for thine honour; for the Lord shall sell Sisera into the hand of a woman. And Deborah arose, and went with Barak to Kedesh. Judges 4:8-9

Deborah prophesied that the enemy would be delivered into Barak's hand but his response showed a lack of faith and a lack of understanding. He refused to go on this mission without her company.

Barak knew that Deborah carried the power of God so heavily. He figured that if she went with him, God would be there also. He wanted Deborah's anointing to be there with him in the midst of his battles. What he didn't realize was that he had an anointing of his own. He was trusting more in the woman of God, than in God Himself. What he didn't understand is that God was calling him to a personal relationship. God wanted him to learn to trust and depend on Him alone.

Instead of taking an immediate step of obedient faith he put a condition on God's call over his life.

Deborah then predicted Sisera's death would be wrought by a woman and that there would be no glory for Barak. It was a rebuke. She pretty much said that if he wanted a woman to go with him, then a woman would get the victory. Of course her prophecy came true but she wasn't the one who would get her hands dirty in the battle.

There was another woman who would make herself available for the work of God. Nevertheless, Deborah arose to accompany Barak on his mission.

And Barak called Zebulun and Naphtali to Kedesh; and he went up with ten thousand men at his feet: and Deborah went up with him. Judges 4:10

After the rebuke from Deborah, Barak still proceeded with the mission. He was willing to go out and serve, and toil, and risk his neck with no glory, nor recognition for himself. In this we can see growth. We could see his faith being developed in humility. Without the need of recognition nor reward he got up and did what he was called to do. Perhaps this is one of the reasons why Barak is listed in the book of Hebrews as a hero of the faith.

In reality we should all have the same kind of attitude about our service to the to the Lord. It's not about acknowledgement, praise or reward. Being that we are servants we should be giving up the need to be honored or recognized. We ought to be willing to serve even if we go unnoticed. That is exactly what Barak did here.

He humbly stepped into his calling by recruiting a plentiful multitude of 10,000 soldiers from Zebulun and Naphtali and he marched out to battle in Kedesh. Deborah went with him and the

Lord did exactly as He promised. He drew out the enemy to meet Barak by the river Kishon with his chariots and his troops.

And Deborah said unto Barak, Up; for this is the day in which the Lord hath delivered Sisera into thine hand: is not the Lord gone out before thee? So Barak went down from mount Tabor, and ten thousand men after him. Judges 4:14

As the enemy was drawn out, Deborah began to rally the troops. She assured the people that the Lord had gone out before them and that He would deliver the enemy into their hands. This motivated Barak to lead the ten thousand soldiers down from Mount Tabor into a victorious battle.

And the Lord discomfited Sisera, and all his chariots, and all his host, with the edge of the sword before Barak; so that Sisera lighted down off his chariot, and fled away on his feet. But Barak pursued after the chariots, and after the host, unto Harosheth of the Gentiles: and all the host of Sisera fell upon the edge of the sword; and there was not a man left. Judges 4:15-16

Barak was outnumbered and outgunned by his enemies. Yet the Lord was on his side so not even the odds could stand against him.

As the battle raged on the Lord embarrassed Sisera and all his troops with the of the edge of the sword. The edge of the sword represents the prophetic word of God that was brought forth by Deborah. Barak was cleaving to the word she spoke to him about the victory. He accepted it as the truth. He went out to battle trusting in the Lord and his faith was developed in the process. He put his trust in the Name of the Lord and because of it he was able to rise up and stand firm.

It was because of his faith that the Lord began moving on his behalf. Mountains began to crumble and his enemies scattered before him. There was not a man left of all those that rose up against him in battle. Those that followed Sisera fell by the edge of the sword. They placed their trust in iron chariots, in horses, and in the strength of the troops but they were brought to their knees in shame.

Howbeit Sisera fled away on his feet to the tent of Jael the wife of Heber the Kenite: for there was peace between Jabin the king of Hazor and the house of Heber the Kenite. And Jael went out to meet Sisera, and said unto him, Turn in, my lord, turn in to me; fear not. And when he had turned in unto her into the tent, she covered him with a mantle. And he said unto her, Give me, I pray thee, a little water to drink; for I am thirsty. And she opened a bottle of milk, and gave him drink, and covered him. Again he said unto her, Stand in the door of the tent, and it shall be, when any man doth come and enquire of thee, and say, Is there any man here? that thou shalt say, No. Judges 4:17-20

Sisera knew that his chances of survival were slim to none. He was getting trampled on by the children of Israel. In an attempt to escape the sword, he jumped off of his chariot and fled on foot to the tent of Jael.

The Bible mentions Jael as the wife of Heber. Once again this is referring to the head of her household. Jael's husband Heber was at peace with Jabin the king of Hazor and therefore Sisera thought that it would be safe to run to her tent and hide out there.

Since Heber was at peace with Jabin it would be accurate to say that he was allied with the same evil and attached to the same sin that had the nation of Israel under subjection. Jabin and Sisera represent the sin and the evil that was dominating Israel at the time. Therefore if Heber was at peace with Jabin then he was more than likely walking in darkness too.

Jael greeted Sisera upon arrival with gentle words. She invited him in by assuring him that there was nothing to fear. She showed him hospitality to the point where he felt comfortable enough to relax. She gave him a blanket and when he asked for water she gave him milk.

Some scholars believe that she was concealing her true thoughts and motives towards him the whole time. Jael was not an Israelite but she was hand-picked by God to do His work. This goes to show that God can choose, and use anybody to be a part of His perfect plan.

It took courage for her to do what she did next. At the prompting of the Holy Spirit she set her fears aside and stepped into the role she was meant to play.

Then Jael Heber's wife took a nail of the tent, and took an hammer in her hand, and went softly unto him, and smote the nail into his temples, and fastened it into the ground: for he was fast asleep and weary. So he died. Judges 4:21

When evil spirits are cast out of people they roam through dry places seeking rest. We can see this taking place as Sisera was cast out of Israel and tried to find rest in Jael's tent. She may have welcomed it at first but when she recognized the darkness and the filth that was in her home she slayed it with no hesitation.

Despite the fact that her husband was at peace with Jabin, she made the ultimate decision to side with the Most High God and to put in work as well. She grabbed the workman's hammer and drove a nail through the enemy's head. She didn't have a sword handy. She simply had to use the tools provided for the work that needed to be done.

Some Bible scholars believe that she was experienced with the hammer from putting up tents with tent pegs. Therefore, it is believed that she developed this skill for the specific reason of doing God's work.

While she was building tents God was equipping her for the task of slaying Sisera. She put her hand to the nail and her right hand to the workman's hammer and pierced the nail right through his temples.

Now this goes to show that when the woman puts her hand to the work of God she too can bring a great victory, not only to her household, but also to the people God. Yes, God uses women to do great things too. He wants to use men, women, and children on His mission to reach all men, women, and children.

The victory of Jael also took place to fulfill the prophetic word of God brought forth by Deborah. She prophesied to Barak that a the glory of this battle would go to a woman.

God knew of this event long before it ever took place. He revealed it to Deborah, and Deborah spoke it to Barak. God knew that Jael would make herself available to do His bidding. He saw her courage, and He saw her obedience long before any of it ever took place.

And, behold, as Barak pursued Sisera, Jael came out to meet him, and said unto him, Come, and I will shew thee the man whom thou seekest. And when he came into her tent, behold, Sisera lay dead, and the nail was in his temples. So God subdued on that day Jabin the king of Canaan before the children of Israel. And the hand of the children of Israel prospered, and prevailed against Jabin the king of Canaan, until they had destroyed Jabin king of Canaan. Judges 4:22-24

Barak must have seen the direction in which Sisera fled because after he was finished dealing with the troops he pursued him.

When he arrived at Jael's tent she greeted him. She was anxious to show him the man whom he sought. She knew very well for whom he was looking. She invited him into her tent and he saw Sisera lying dead with the nail still in his head.

Not only was Jabin's commanding officer killed that day but Jabin was also destroyed by the hand of Israel.

Deborah did her part, Barak did his, the troops had a role to play, and so did Jael. None of these characters had to be the whole story. They were all a part of a great company and they rejoiced in that.

The diversity of gifts and callings were brought together for the perfecting of the saints, the work of the ministry and the edification of the body. We see unity and growth in this chapter. One faith, one hope, one God. That is what this story is all about. It shows how faith is developed in the company of others.

Israel was set free from bondage that day. Heber got to whiteness victory in his house because of the obedience and courage of his wife Jael. The whole nation was able to celebrate in this victory because their enemy was slain.

In chapter 5 of the book of Judges there is a song written by Deborah and Barak. They praised God for avenging Israel by the hands of those who willingly offered themselves. He avenged Israel by the hands of those that made themselves available. They gave praise to God for all He did in, and through the lives of those that participated in the mission. The song makes mention of how Deborah arose as a mother in Israel and it makes mention of how Jael was considered to be blessed above women.

Judges 5:30 also gives us a better understanding of Sisera's character. It speaks of his intentions to divide the spoils of God's people and abusing the women whom he captured. He defiled women and therefore he was judged by one.

Keep in mind that Sisera represents the sin and the evil that held Israel under subjection at the time. If he was greedy for gain and abusive to women then that is the kind of sinful nature that the people were subject to at the time.

That same spirit still exists to this day. It is a spirit that influences the ruthless nature of abusing members of the opposite sex. It has been known to work through men and women where they will be abusive physically, mentally, or emotionality to their significant other. To those who have had an issue in this area of life you can change. God has called you to battle against it. If you make a stand against it God will deliver it into your hands: "Awake, awake, Deborah: awake, awake, utter a song: arise, Barak, and lead thy captivity captive, thou son of Abinoam" (Judges 5:12)

And the children of Israel did evil in the sight of the LORD: and the LORD delivered them into the hand of Midian seven years. Judges 6:1

The forty years of rest that followed Israel's victory over Jabin and his army came to an end in due course.

Once again the Israelites entered into the sinful phase of their repeated cycle. They did what was evil in the eyes of the Lord and so the Lord handed them over to Midian for a duration of seven years.

As Israel returned to their sinful behavior they found that their troubles awaited therein. The Lord was not willing to let His children enjoy their sin, nor was He willing to allow them to be successful in it. Therefore He brought them trouble by the hands of their enemies.

And the hand of Midian prevailed against Israel: and because of the Midianites the children of Israel made them the dens which are in the mountains, and caves, and strongholds. Judges 6:2

We have come to the conclusion that if we decide to live sinfully we should be expecting to suffer on account of it.

It is true that all believers will undergo suffering even when living righteously. On the other hand we will also suffer for doing wrong. This is a different kind of suffering.

When we suffer righteously Christ provides the strength to endure. We find purpose in it, and we have victory in it. But the suffering that comes from wrongdoing is the type of suffering that will bring somebody low. This type of suffering will break a person down mentally and emotionally. The purpose of it is to bring God's children to repentance. Those who have experienced it will understand the difference.

The Lord strengthened the hands of Midian so they prevailed against Israel. When God strengthens the hands of our enemies against us we have no chances of overcoming. We will not see victory until we surrender to His will. We can't expect to put up a fight against the Almighty One. Our hands are too short to box with God.

This is why Midian was able to overpower and subdue the children of Israel. The Midianites became too strong to stand against.

The question is, who are the Midianites? And what do they represent?

In Genesis chapter 25:1-2 we find that the patriarch Abraham took another wife after the death of Sarah. This woman went by the name of Keturah. According to this scripture she bore him six children namely Zimran, and Jokshan, and Medan, and Midian, and Ishbak, and Shuah.

The Midianites were the descendants of Midian which was Abraham's fourth son from Keturah. This means that they were actually the relatives of Israel. Both were seeds brought forth from Abraham.

Nevertheless, only Israel was considered the covenant people of God. Jael the woman who slayed Sisera came from the genealogy of the Midianites and Jethro the father in law of Moses as well. Other than that the Midianites were confrontational towards Israel.

And so it was, when Israel had sown, that the Midianites came up, and the Amalekites, and the children of the east, even they came up against them; and they encamped against them, and destroyed the increase of the earth, till thou come unto Gaza, and left no sustenance for Israel, neither sheep, nor ox, nor ass. For they came up with their cattle and their tents, and they came as grasshoppers for multitude; for both they and their camels were without number: and they entered into the land to destroy it. And Israel was greatly impoverished because of the Midianites; and the children of Israel cried unto the LORD. Judges 6: 3-6

They didn't just take their crops to devour them; they destroyed them. All the fruit and vegetables were cut down and laid waste. Even the grass was brought to ruin.

In other words the Israelites were reaping destruction: "whoever sows to please their flesh, from the flesh will reap destruction" (Galatians 6:8). The truth of the matter is that Israel got carried away sowing to the flesh. They did whatever felt pleasing to their mortal bodies. They were indulging in sin. The result was a harvest of corruption. Those who live according to the flesh should not expect anything other than misery and destruction when choosing to walk this path.

Those who spend their time chasing pleasures to gratify themselves will reap destruction. The mortal body will literally go through a dying and perishing state on account of sin. The Lord was showing Israel a reflection of their own lives by destroying everything around them. They were headed to an eternal state of destruction.

Without repentance their end would result in a separation between them and God forever. This is opposed to the harvest of eternal life for those who sow to the spirit. Hell is destruction.

Yet God works in a mysterious way. He gave His people a taste of destruction here on earth so that they would realize what they were headed for and turn from it.

The Midianites waited until the last moment to destroy the work that Israel sweated for. There are many who have experienced this evil in their own lives. They choose to sow to the flesh. They chase the things which seem to be pleasurable and they reap a harvest of destruction.

It was when Israel had sown that the enemy came up against them. After all their hard work they expected to receive a plentiful harvest but the enemy encamped against them and destroyed all that Israel worked for. It's like working so hard to get a paycheck only to find a hole in your pocket when it arrives.

The Midianites also destroyed the livestock of Israel. The sheep, the oxen, and the asses were all gone. The whole land was devastated and the inhabitants thereof were deprived of the necessities of life.

With only one glimpse of the scene during this time you would see the devil's trademark all over it (destruction). He comes to steal, kill, and destroy. That is exactly what happened to the crops and the livestock of Israel. They were stolen, killed, and destroyed.

The Midianites brought their own cattle and tents and took up residence in the land of Israel. This is exactly what evil spirits aim to do in the lives of God's people. They focus on infiltrating, destroying, and taking up residence.

The sole purpose of the Midianite spirit is to destroy the increase of God's people. Those who sow to the flesh, will experience this spirit.

The Midianites came as locusts for multitude; for both they and their camels were without number.

Throughout scripture you will find how the Lord sends the locusts to devour the land of all those who are outside of His will. Perhaps you can see the metaphor that is being used in this verse.

Israel was greatly impoverished because of the swarming enemy who devoured their land. They were made poor and brought low to a pitiful state.

Many of us who walk confidently in the spirit now have been there before. We have been in a state of misery and defeat. At the very bottom we find that there is nowhere else to look but up.

Towards heaven. Towards a God who is high and lifted up and in Him we find hope.

The children of Israel cried unto the Lord and this is where they begin sowing to the spirit. This is the way from which we can all be saved from our troubles. This is how we can reap an everlasting life. Not just calling out during troublesome times but continually staying close to God and living in surrender to His will.

(2 Chronicles 7:13-14 NIV "When I shut up the heavens so that there is no rain, or command locusts to devour the land or send a plague among my people, if my people, who are called by my name, will humble themselves and pray and seek my face and turn from their wicked ways, then I will hear from heaven, and I will forgive their sin and will heal their land.)

(Joel 2:25-27 And I will restore to you the years that the locust hath eaten, the cankerworm, and the caterpillar, and the palmerworm, my great army which I sent among you. And ye shall eat in plenty, and be satisfied, and praise the name of the Lord your God, that hath dealt wondrously with you: and my people shall never be ashamed. And ye shall know that I am in the midst of Israel, and that I am the Lord your God, and none else: and my people shall never be ashamed.)

In Judges 6 we find that the Lord sends a prophet before he ever sends a deliverer. The prophet was sent to explain the reason why they were in this mess in the first place. They were stuck in idolatry.

Sowing to the flesh is another form of idolatry. It could be as simple as putting your belly before God. The severe punishment that Israel had received through the hands of Midian came from a deep form of idolatry through the feeding of one's flesh.

This behavior seen today when people dedicate themselves to the addiction of hard drugs. Those that spend their time feeding their flesh with the pleasure of getting high end up suffering from lack of increase.

The drug becomes their God and the God of the Bible is pushed aside. Yet the God of the Bible is the only true God and He is jealous when His people spend their lives chasing things other than Himself for pleasure. This results in chastisement.

And it came to pass, when the children of Israel cried unto the Lord because of the Midianites, That the Lord sent a prophet unto the children of Israel, which said unto them, Thus saith the Lord God of Israel, I brought you up from Egypt, and brought you forth out of the house of bondage; And I delivered you out of the hand of the Egyptians, and out of the hand of all that oppressed you, and drove them out from before you, and gave you their land; And I said unto you, I am the Lord your God; fear not the gods of the Amorites, in whose land ye dwell: but ye have not obeyed my voice. Judges 6:7-10

And there came an angel of the Lord, and sat under an oak which was in Ophrah, that pertained unto Joash the Abiezrite: and his son Gideon threshed wheat by the winepress, to hide it from the Midianites. Judges 6:11

Angels are ministering spirits, sent forth to minister for them who shall be heirs of salvation (Hebrews 1:14). They come to offer up assistance to those who belong to God. They are also messengers, and guardians to the people of the Lord.

This particular angel is also thought to be an incarnation of the Son of God. He sat under an oak which was located in Ophrah. The oak belonged to Joash the Abiezrite. The oak tree can be considered a symbol of God's righteousness. In the book of Isaiah chapter 61 verse 3 you will find that God's people may be called oaks of righteousness, the planting of the Lord.

The Bible tells us that the Lord also appeared to Abraham by the oaks of Mamre. This scene also makes mention of three heavenly beings in human form yet it specifically states that the Lord appeared to Abraham. Therefore some believe that one of these beings was also the incarnate Son of God.

While the angel sat under the oak, Gideon the son of Joash

threshed wheat by the winepress. Threshing is the process of loosening the edible part of grain from the chaff. The winepress was not the ideal place to do this kind of work but Gideon was threshing wheat where he could hide it from the Midianites. He was afraid but he still had the courage to do something about his situation.

If he would have threshed on the threshing floor he would have been spotted by the enemy. This would have put his life in danger. He stood no chance to fight against the Midianites because the Lord had strengthened them. Yet Gideon refused to sit back and let his family go hungry. Despite the circumstances he was doing what needed to be done.

How else would his loved ones survive? How else did they survive throughout the seven years of poverty and oppression?

Gideon was doing all that he could under the circumstances he was given. He was working with what he had. He turned the winepress into a threshing floor. Sometimes we have to learn to do the same thing.

Sometimes we have to turn the curb into an altar, the jail cell into a prayer closet, or the street corner into a pulpit. The enemy doesn't expect that.

There is a place where even our enemy would not expect us to be in times of oppression. The enemy expects us to give up and forfeit our lives along with everything else that belongs to us. He plans to make a threshing floor in our own heart so that he can sift us as wheat.

He doesn't expect the downtrodden to be in prayer. He doesn't expect the hurting to be entertaining angels. He doesn't expect the oppressed to consider the miracles of the Lord. That is exactly what we will find Gideon doing as he threshed wheat in the winepress.

And the angel of the Lord appeared unto him, and said unto him, The Lord is with thee, thou mighty man of valour. And Gideon said unto him, Oh my Lord, if the LORD be with us, why then is all this befallen us? and where be all his miracles which our fathers told us of, saying, Did not the LORD bring us up from Egypt? but now the LORD hath forsaken us, and delivered us into the hands of the Midianites. Judges 6:12-13

The angel showed up to reveal the purpose and the calling of Gideon. It could be that the children of Israel took heed to the words of the prophet and began the process of repentance. Therefore the Lord sent His angel to ordain the next judge in whom He would use to bring deliverance to them.

The angel assured Gideon that the Lord was on his side. There was work that needed to be done and Gideon was the man in whom God delighted to use. God called him a mighty man of valor. A title that fit the description for the job that would soon be filled. The Lord was calling Gideon a warrior and He was willing to advance him into one.

Gideon responded by asking the angel, "if God is with us, why then is all this befallen us"(v.13)? He wanted to know why they were suffering and why they were in such a pitiful condition.

He wasn't considering the evil of his people, otherwise he would have known the answer to that question. Israel did evil in the sight of the Lord and that's why they were under severe punishment. It was their sin that got them into this mess.

Gideon was looking at the problem but failed to consider the root cause of it. He was looking at their condition. He saw the their poverty and brokenness.

He proceeded to ask about all the miracles of God which were told to him by his fathers, saying, Did not the Lord bring us up from Egypt (v.13)? He considered the miracles that were done for Israel in past times when God was with them. People were set free and delivered out of bondage. People had victory over their enemies.

At this point in time there were no miracles, no deliverance, and no victory taking place. There was no evidence that the Lord was on their side. This led Gideon to believe that the Lord had forsaken him and his people.

Just because trouble arrives, it does not mean that God has

forsaken you. God, in all His sovereignty, delivered Israel into the hands of the Midianites but there was a purpose for it. God had a plan for their salvation.

This punishment would lead to their repentance at which point God would intervene by raising up a deliverer to save them from the enemy. In this particular case Gideon was the man who was hand-picked by God to bring this deliverance.

And the Lord looked upon him, and said, Go in this thy might, and thou shalt save Israel from the hand of the Midianites: have not I sent thee? Judges 6:14

While Gideon is entertaining this angel the Lord looked upon him and said go in this thy might. Due to this verse many people believe that this angel was the incarnate Son of God. The Lord looked on Gideon either from heaven or from the eyes of this angel and said Go in this thy might, and thou shalt save Israel from the hand of the Midianites.

These were the instructions that he received to deliver Israel. Go in this thy might. Don't go in your own strength but go in this; The commission and the authority I have given you. This is thy might. Not human strength but divine power.

The Lord is your strength. Strengthen yourself in Him and put on the full armor of God. His strength is made perfect in your weaknesses. If He has called you to war He will empower you to be a warrior. God will always empower us to do what He calls us to do.

And he said unto him, Oh my Lord, wherewith shall I save Israel? behold, my family is poor in Manasseh, and I am the least in my father's house. Judges 6:15

Gideon responded with a lack of confidence. His low self-esteem is portrayed as he gives a description of his family and himself.

Many people today have also formed a pretty low opinion about the character of Gideon. Due to the fact that Gideon was hiding in the winepress from the Midianites many say that he was a coward. Many say that he was afraid, timid, and doubtful.

Perhaps many of his own people made him feel this way about himself. It is important that we do not let other people's opinions fabricate our lifestyle. It could be dangerous to believe what others believe about us, especially when they are in a defeated state themselves.

Truthfully, it is not what we think about ourselves, nor what anybody else thinks about us that counts. It is what God thinks about us that matters. The Lord called Gideon a mighty man of valor. Despite what anybody thinks about you or even what you think about yourself, you are chosen, you are loved, and you are exactly who God says you are.

It's important that we never get to thinking that we are better than anybody else. There has to be a balance. We must learn to be humble. There is no respect of persons so we should not get carried away in pride nor conceit. Don't get big headed.

The Bible tells us not to think more highly about ourselves then we ought to, yet we should never think any lower neither. There is nothing more precious than to know you are a child of the Most High God. It has been said "we never know who we are till we find out who's we are." Once we find out who we are in Christ we can learn how to esteem ourselves more properly.

The Bible says that you are fearfully and wonderfully made. You are created in His image and therefore you are a reflection of who He really is. You are a royal priesthood. So precious that the Lord keeps you as the Apple of His eye.

Now if the Lord thinks this way about you then why would you think any less about yourself? If the Lord is calling you a mighty man/ woman of valor then you should believe it. Just keep a proper balance on how you see yourself. Stay humble but be confident. This is just something to keep in mind. It's not just about how we view God that matters but it is also important to know how God views us. Grab ahold of this concept and come to a better understanding of your place in service to Him.

Believe that God can and will use you to do big things. There is no limit to what God can do through you. He will move you from fear to faith and in the process use you to change the world around you.

And the Lord said unto him, Surely I will be with thee, and thou shalt smite the Midianites as one man. Judges 6:16

The Lord reassured Gideon that He would be with him to help him on his journey, to strengthen him on his way, and to uphold him on his mission. When the Lord calls you to do any particular assignment He will also be with you to assist you in it. He doesn't just watch you fight from the sidelines, He gets involved. The involvement of the sovereign Lord in our lives should be enough to motivate anyone to proceed with the mission no matter how intimidating it may seem. If God is with us then that means He is also for us and what could possibly stand against us.

The Midianites were as grasshoppers for multitude yet the Lord told Gideon that he would strike them down as one man. It is so much easier to look at the enemy as one person than as a multitude. We have so many problems that we deal with each day. It would be nice if we could turn all our problems into one issue and get rid of it all in one blow.

This is what God was willing to do for Israel at the time. No more living in caves, no more losing their crops, no more losing their livestock, no more poverty and no more Midianites. All this would come to a stop at the end of this one war.

And he said unto him, If now I have found grace in thy sight, then shew me a sign that thou talkest with me. Depart not hence, I pray thee, until I come unto thee, and bring forth my present, and set it before thee. And he said, I will tarry until thou come again. And Gideon went in, and made ready a kid, and unleavened cakes of an ephah of flour: the flesh he put in a basket, and he put the broth in a pot, and brought it out unto him under the oak, and presented it. And the angel of God said unto him, Take the flesh and the unleavened cakes, and lay them upon this rock, and pour out the broth. And he did so. Then the angel of the Lord put forth the end of the staff that was in his hand, and touched the flesh and the unleavened cakes; and there rose up fire out of the rock, and consumed the flesh and the unleavened cakes. Then the angel of the Lord departed out of his sight. Judges 6:17-21

Gideon asked for a sign from God and he received one. Asking for a sign from God can be sinful when it is done with the wrong motives. Jesus said, "A wicked and adulterous generation looks for a sign, but none will be given it except the sign of Jonah (Mathew 16:4 NIV)." Gideon's intentions were not evil and adulterous, otherwise no sign would've been given to him. Gideon asked for a sign to confirm that he was hearing from God and not from a mere man nor devil.

Apparently, Gideon's ears were not yet familiar with the voice of God because he didn't recognize it when it came to him.

Gideon was lacking in faith and therefore he asked for a sign. A person usually asks for a sign to get direction or confirmation in times of uncertainty. In this particular case Gideon just wanted to make sure he was getting these instructions from the right source. The scripture tells us not to believe every spirit, but to test the spirits to see whether they are from God (1 John 4:1). This is exactly what Gideon was doing when he asked for a sign. He was testing the Spirit.

Gideon asked the angel not to depart until he brought forth an offering to him. The angel agreed. Keep in mind that Gideon was making an offering even out of his poverty. His whole nation was in poverty because of Midian. Yet even in his poverty Gideon brought forth a meal.

The offering that Gideon prepared was more than likely a meal that was intended to refresh the angel but it was set on fire. This was a sign to show Gideon that the man whom he spoke to was not a man that needed meat for refreshment. The angel also disappeared. Setting the offering on fire was a sign and there was a meaning behind it.

The offering that was set to fire became a burnt offering which is equivalent to a sacrifice. God was communicating to Gideon through this sign to show him what type of offering He wanted from him. He wanted Gideon to turn his offering into a sacrifice.

The Bible tells us to offer our bodies as a living sacrifice holy and pleasing to God. This is our true and proper worship towards God. The flesh that was set on fire is metaphorical to the body (Romans 12:1). The Lord wants us to offer bodies up for the purpose of serving Him. God was calling Gideon to live a life of complete surrender, devotion, and commitment.

The apostle Paul mentions burning the body in 1 Corinthians 13:3 ("And though I bestow all my goods to feed the poor, and though I give my body to be burned, and have not charity, it profiteth me nothing.") This means that when we offer our bodies up for our reasonable service to God we have to be doing it wholeheartedly. There has to be love towards God, towards others, and towards self or the offering is no more an offering.

The burnt offering represents us giving ourselves to the Lord in service. A sin offering is quite different because it represents the atonement for sin. Jesus-Christ became the sin offering for this world so that we can all be forgiven and reunited with God.

And when Gideon perceived that he was an angel of the Lord, Gideon said, Alas, O Lord God! for because I have seen an angel of the Lord face to face. And the Lord said unto him, Peace be unto thee; fear not: thou shalt not die. Then Gideon built an altar there unto the Lord, and called it Jehovahshalom: unto this day it is yet in Ophrah of the Abiezrites. Judges 6:22-24

The sign was enough to open up the eyes of Gideon so that he would recognize the angel. This is how we know that the angel came in human form: "Do not forget to show hospitality to strangers, for by so doing some people have shown hospitality to angels without knowing it"(Hebrews 13:2 NIV).

Gideon thought he was going to die after this experience but the Lord gave him peace by assuring him that he would not die. Therefore, Gideon built an altar and named it Jehovah Shalom. God gives us peace.

And it came to pass the same night, that the Lord said unto him, Take thy father's young bullock, even the second bullock of seven years old, and throw down the altar of Baal that thy father hath, and cut down the grove that is by it: Judges 6:25

This was Gideon's first assignment. God told him to start with tearing down the altar of Baal that his father had built, and to proceed with cutting down the grove that stood next to it.

In those times the altar was the place where sacrifices were offered and incense was burned in worship. Gideon's father had an altar where sacrifices were made to Baal. This was an abomination in God's eyes. This was the very reason why they were under punishment in the first place. Therefore, the Lord told Gideon to tear down this altar where sacrifices were made unto this idol.

The grove was also to be cut down. It was a small wood without underbrush that was usually carved into an image of the idols being worshipped.

This is a good starting point for any new convert. God wants us to tear down any altars within our own lives where sacrifices may have been made to any other than Himself.

Many people sacrifice their time and energy on the altar of addiction. There are people who sacrifice their freedom for gang reputation. There is also people who have sacrificed time that they could spend with family on the altar of career advancement.

It is important that we consider the sacrifices that we have made to anything other than God and recognize when we are stuck in idol worship. We have to stop making sacrifices that tend to rob God of His worship.

If there was ever any place in our own lives where we may have made sacrifices to dumb idols then the Holy Spirit will prompt us to tear down the altars thereof. These are the first steps to leadership in our Christian walk. We have to make a bold statement that we will no longer partake in idolatry. We are not going to stand for the wickedness of it nor will not we allow it to go on.

We need to clean house in order to start fresh. In order for our repentance to be absolute we must tear down any other existing altars.

Somebody has to step up and take charge in leadership so that other people can do the same. Perhaps the Lord is asking you to apply this word.

Tear down the altar of Baal. Make a bold statement and stand firm. Rise up men and women of God and take the right direction so that others may follow.

And build an altar unto the Lord thy God upon the top of this rock, in the ordered place, and take the second bullock, and offer a burnt sacrifice with the wood of the grove which thou shalt cut down. Judges 6:26

Once the altar of Baal was torn down, Gideon was told to build an alter unto the Lord. He was told to use the wood from the grove in order to burn the second bullock as a sacrifice on it.

This brings confirmation to the sign that the angel gave to Gideon. The Lord was asking Gideon to build an altar and make a burnt sacrifice to Him. The burnt sacrifice represents the offering of oneself to God.

Once we have torn down the pagan altars in our own lives we can proceed to build an altar to God. A place where we can worship God. A place where we can burn incense and offer sacrifices unto Him.

The burning of incense combined with the burning of sacrifices represents the merging of prayer and devotion. We can come to the altar to pray and offer ourselves as a living sacrifice unto God. This is what the Lord was calling Gideon to do and this is what he wants from us as well. He gave us life and the least we could do is honor him with it. He also gave himself on the cross for our sins.

They say there is nothing that we can do to pay God back for all He has done for us, and this is true, but He will accept it when we devote our lives to serving Him. We need to stop giving our strength and our time to anything other than God. We have to recognize when we focus too much time and energy on anything besides Him. He is a Jealous God.

Then Gideon took ten men of his servants, and did as the Lord had said unto him: and so it was, because he feared his father's household, and the men of the city, that he could not do it by day, that he did it by night. Judges 6:27

The ten men that Gideon took were his servants. It was necessary to take all this manpower for the task of tearing down the altar, and the grove, along with building an altar unto God.

This was a big job for Gideon. He also knew that his father's house and the men of the city would be angry and rise against him for doing this. He feared that if he made his move by day the people of the city would intervene and prevent him from accomplishing his task. It was a logical and prudent choice to make his move at night.

Many people see Gideon as cowardly because of this. Perhaps his faith wasn't yet that bold. The underlining factor is that Gideon did what the Lord had told him to do. He was obedient. He trusted God, knowing that the people of the city would still be angry with him.

In like manner we must always be willing to do what the Lord tells us to do. No matter what other people might think or how they might react. If the Lord places it in our hearts to do something or say something then we must act with obedience no matter the consequences.

And when the men of the city arose early in the morning, behold, the altar of Baal was cast down, and the grove was cut down that was by it, and the second bullock was offered upon the altar that was built. And they said one to another, Who hath done this thing? And when they enquired and asked, they said, Gideon the son of Joash hath done this thing. Then the men of the city said unto Joash, Bring out thy son, that he may die: because he hath cast down the altar of Baal, and because he hath cut down the grove that was by it. And Joash said unto all that stood against him, Will ye plead for Baal? will ye save him? he that will plead for him, let him be put to death whilst it is yet morning: if he be a god, let him plead for himself, because one hath cast down his altar. Therefore on that day he called him Jerubbaal, saying, Let Baal plead against him, because he hath thrown down his altar. Judges 6:28-32

The men of the city wanted to kill Gideon when they discovered that he had torn down the altar of Baal. Joash did what any parent would do under the circumstances. He protected his child.

The altar of Baal had belonged to Joash in the first place. Apparently he was no longer dedicated to the idol. He must've recognized that there was no power in it.

If the idol did have power, Gideon wouldn't have been able to destroy its altar. Therefore Joash said "if Baal really is a god then let him be the one to defend himself. Let him be the one to strike Gideon for doing this work"(v.31).

In all reality it was the hand of God protecting Gideon at this point. No harm came to him because God was with him.

Gideon also received the name of Jerubbaal because he was bold enough to contend with Baal. His father gave him the name while saying 'let Baal plead against him."

The Lord had already begun to stir up the heart of Joash through the obedience of Gideon. You would be amazed at how God will stir up the hearts of others through your obedience. It is through the obedience of a sincere heart that lives get touched.

Then all the Midianites and the Amalekites and the children of the east were gathered together, and went over, and pitched in the valley of Jezreel. But the Spirit of the LORD came upon Gideon, and he blew a trumpet; and Abiezer was gathered after him. Judges 6:33-34

It was harvest time, and so the enemy had returned. The Midianites had gathered together with their allies and encamped against the Israelites once again to destroy their increase.

The Spirit of the Lord came upon Gideon and motivated him to sound the trumpet. To call the men to arms. It was time to fight back.

The Abiezrites were the first to gather. These were the men that Gideon described as the weakest in the tribe of Manasseh. He also sent messengers throughout all Manasseh and the whole tribe gathered after him. He also sent messengers to Asher, Zebulun, and Naphtali; and they gathered together as well.

The influence was there. The leadership was there. An exceedingly great army was gathered at the sound of the trumpet.

And Gideon said unto God, If thou wilt save Israel by mine hand, as thou hast said, Behold, I will put a fleece of wool in the floor; and if the dew be on the fleece only, and it be dry upon all the earth beside, then shall I know that thou wilt save Israel by mine hand, as thou hast said. Judges 6:36-37

There was still a bit of doubt lingering in Gideon's heart. So he asked for another sign. He basically said, "Lord, if you are really going to do what you said you would do then show me another sign."

The first time that Gideon asked for a sign, it was to confirm the voice of God. He wanted to make sure that it was God who spoke to him. This time Gideon wanted to make sure that God was really going to use him to bring deliverance to his people. After all, this was a big deal, right?

Who would think that out of all the people in Israel, God would choose Gideon for such a great deed. In like manner, God has also chosen you to do something great. Great things come with great challenges.

We must learn to put trust in God and take Him at His Word. Without trust and belief people need an endless amount of confirmation: "Without faith it is impossible to please God" (Hebrews 11:16). Gideon is frowned upon for this very reason. What we don't realize is that all of us were like Gideon at one point or another.

Nobody starts the race with such great faith. Some of us start with little to no faith. When we come to God we are broken. We've been hurt too many times and we have trust issues. We've been let down by too many people to fully trust anyone. We have scars from all the broken promises.

God knows that and therefore He uses signs and wonders to build our faith. Jesus put it this way, "Unless you see signs and wonders, you will not believe" (John 4:48). Therefore we know that signs are given so that people would grow in the faith.

The 12 disciples witnessed the signs and wonders of Jesus first hand and they still had to ask Jesus to increase their faith. Gideon had really small faith even after the first sign that was given. Even after the Holy Spirit had already come upon him. He still needed more confirmation.

God is faithful and we can trust Him. Yet we still have a tendency to be doubtful. We do not need any more confirmation about our calling than what God has already given. Sometimes we just have to refresh ourselves in what God has already told us and trust Him.

And it was so: for he rose up early on the morrow, and thrust the fleece together, and wringed the dew out of the fleece, a bowl full of water. And Gideon said unto God, Let not thine anger be hot against me, and I will speak but this once: let me prove, I pray thee, but this once with the fleece; let it now be dry only upon the fleece, and upon all the ground let there be dew. And God did so that night: for it was dry upon the fleece only, and there was dew on all the ground. Judges 6:38-40

How many signs do we need before we can take God at His word? Gideon knew that he was pushing it because he said "let not thine anger be hot against me." He wanted one more sign. A third one.

It was a lack of faith that produced the desire for another sign. Yet, God still gave him another. Perhaps it was because of the obedience that Gideon had already shown when he threw down the altars of Baal. Or perhaps it was because God had already known that Gideon would eventually grow in his faith and that is what motivated Him to give Gideon another sign.

There is also a deeper message that comes with this sign. The fleece and the ground represents the lamb of God and the church. When the dew fell from heaven and only landed on the fleece it symbolizes how Christ would take all the punishment for our sin, such that none would fall upon us. When the dew that fell from heaven was wetting the floor only, it symbolizes the righteousness of God being poured out onto this world, because of what Christ would do at the cross.

Then Jerubbaal, who is Gideon, and all the people that were with him, rose up early, and pitched beside the well of Harod: so that the host of the Midianites were on the north side of them, by the hill of Moreh, in the valley. Judges 7:1

It was early in the morning when Jerubbaal (Gideon) and those who gathered with him rose up and encamped beside the well of Harod. The name "Harod" means "trembling. They were positioned in a place where they could see the vast army of Midianite soldiers in the valley below.

Gideon had summoned 32,000 men of war, yet in Judges chapter 8 verse 10 we find that the Midianite army was at least 135,000 men in total. The Midianites and their allies outnumbered Israel by a ratio of more than four to one.

From where the Israelites stood, they could see that the enemy was far bigger than they. This is the place where fear began to grip the hearts of those who did not understand the concept of trusting in God. Perhaps that is why the place was called "the springs of trembling."

Maybe you are not one to struggle with fear, but there always comes a point in life when we have to face some challenges that seem too difficult to handle. Sometimes the adversary is far too big to fight, like a life-threatening sickness that could take your life, or the life of a loved one. Facing the opposition of losing a loved one could bring even the most fearless soul to the place of trembling. This is the place where the whole tribe of Israel was. They were in fear of losing their own lives and the lives of their loved ones.

And the Lord said unto Gideon, The people that are with thee are too many for me to give the Midianites into their hands, lest Israel vaunt themselves against me, saying, Mine own hand hath saved me. Judges 7:2

Gideon's army was already outnumbered by the enemy and yet the Lord told him that there was too many people with him to fight this battle. 32,000 was too many to fight against 135,000.

The Lord knew that if Israel won the battle with all these soldiers that they would think they did it by their own strength. They would go on boasting themselves against Him by saying, "our own hands have saved us." They would try to take credit for the victory. Therefore, the Lord began the process of elimination by reducing the army of Gideon.

Now therefore go to, proclaim in the ears of the people, saying, Whosoever is fearful and afraid, let him return and depart early from mount Gilead. And there returned of the people twenty and two thousand; and there remained ten thousand. Judges 7:3

The reducing of the crowd goes to show that when we are called to fight the Lord's battles, God will begin to remove people from our lives. We come to find that not everyone around us will fight the Lord's battles with us. Not everyone around us will be with us when things get tough.

The fearful ones are usually the first ones to walk away. 22,000 men departed early from mount Gilead because they were afraid to fight the Lord's battles.

There are many people who like to quote the words "if you're scared go to church." But God said "if you're scared go home." The truth of the matter is that it takes a soldier to fight the Lord's battles. It takes a true soldier to carry that cross. It takes a lot of heart to trust God when the situation looks like the one Gideon was facing.

If we learn to fully put our trust in God there will be no room for fear. Perfect love casts out fear. No matter what we may be up against we know that God is sovereign and that He loves us. He has the final say in everything and we can trust Him.

Fear decreases when faith increases. More than two thirds of the people were fearful so the number of soldiers was reduced down to ten thousand men. It would take a lot of faith for these men to stand against an army of 135,000.

And the LORD said unto Gideon, The people are yet too many; bring them down unto the water, and I will try them for thee there: and it shall be, that of whom I say unto thee, This shall go with thee, the same shall go with thee; and of whomsoever I say unto thee, This shall not go with thee, the same shall not go. So he brought down the people unto the water: and the LORD said unto Gideon, Every one that lappeth of the water with his tongue, as a dog lappeth, him shalt thou set by himself; likewise every one that boweth down upon his knees to drink. And the number of them that lapped, putting their hand to their mouth, were three hundred men: but all the rest of the people bowed down upon their knees to drink water. And the LORD said unto Gideon, By the three hundred men that lapped will I save you, and deliver the Midianites into thine hand: and let all the other people go every man unto his place. Judges 7:4-7

At this point, Gideon's army was outnumbered by more than thirteen to one. Yet the Lord said to him "there is still too many people on your side. Bring the army of ten thousand down to the waters to be tested."

They were tested according to how they drank the water. 300 of these men lapped the water like dogs while 9,700 men bowed down upon their knees to drink the water. Those who lapped like a dog would stay and fight while those who got on their knees to drink the water would go home.

The army of Gideon was reduced once again from 10,000 to 300. By reducing Gideon's army, the Lord was really reducing their pride and their self-sufficiency. He didn't want them to take credit for what He did. The glory belongs to God. As a matter of fact, He specifically tells us in Isaiah 48:11 that He will not give His glory to another. God's glory is not something that we should try to steal for ourselves.

Neither does He want us to think that we could do everything on our own strength and sufficiency. If that was the case then God would no longer be needed. But God is needed and He wants us to lean on Him for strength.

That is why we have limitations. That is why He reduced the crowd for Gideon. He wanted them to learn how to fully put their trust in Him and not themselves. We must learn to do the same.

By reducing the crowd He was cutting back their self-dependence. They would know for certain that they could not do this alone.

As the army was decreased so was the manpower behind it. With a decrease of manpower God would be able to give an increase of His power. John the Baptist put it this way: "God must increase, but I must decrease" (John 3:30). Less of me and more of You, Lord. Less of my prideful thoughts, less of my selfish ways, less of my own limited strength, and more of You oh God.

Gideon's army was decreased so that the soldiers would rely more heavily upon God. All the fearful were gone, the proud were resisted, and the arrogant were sent home.

With only 300 men left in the army there would be no way that they could take the credit for winning the battle. Only God can give a victory like this. It can only be done through His divine providence.

So the people took victuals in their hand, and their trumpets: and he sent all the rest of Israel every man unto his tent, and retained those three hundred men: and the host of Midian was beneath him in the valley. Judges 7:8

The 300 men that were chosen to fight the Lord's battle received provisions, and trumpets in their hand from the others. They remained in the hills while the rest of Israel returned home. The host of Midian was beneath them in the valley. We can give attention to the position of both parties to get a better understanding of what happens next.

And it came to pass the same night, that the Lord said unto him, Arise, get thee down unto the host; for I have delivered it into thine hand. But if thou fear to go down, go thou with Phurah thy servant down to the host: And thou shalt hear what they say; and afterward shall thine hands be strengthened to go down unto the host. Then went he down with Phurah his servant unto the outside of the armed men that were in the host. And the Midianites and the Amalekites and all the children of the east lay along in the valley like grasshoppers for multitude; and their camels were without number, as the sand by the sea side for multitude.

And when Gideon was come, behold, there was a man that told a dream unto his fellow, and said, Behold, I dreamed a dream, and, lo, a cake of barley bread tumbled into the host of Midian, and came unto a tent, and smote it that it fell, and overturned it, that the tent lay along. And his fellow answered and said, This is nothing else save the sword of Gideon the son of Joash, a man of Israel: for into his hand hath God delivered Midian, and all the host. And it was so, when Gideon heard the telling of the dream, and the interpretation thereof, that he worshipped, and returned into the host of Israel, and said, Arise; for the Lord hath delivered into your hand the host of Midian. Judges 7:9-15

The Lord told Gideon to go down and attack the host of Midian, but Gideon was still afraid. Therefore, the Lord told him to take his servant Phurah down to the host to eavesdrop on their conversation. It is interesting that Gideon still had fear in his heart even after the first three signs. It is even more interesting that the Lord gave Gideon another one. Gideon didn't ask for this one but the Lord gave it anyways. The sign would strengthen Gideon's hands. It would encourage him and increase his faith so much that people would be reading about it, and preaching about it, thousands of years later, even unto this very day.

As Gideon and his servant Phurah approached the enemy camp, they overheard the conversation between a man and his friend. The man told his friend about a dream he had. A dream about a huge loaf of barley bread tumbling into the Midianite camp, striking a tent so hard that it fell, turned upside down, and laid flat. His friend replied immediately with an interpretation to the dream. He said, "Clearly this is none other than the sword of Gideon the son of Joash, a man of Israel. God has delivered Midian and all the host into his hand."

God had already told Gideon that the host of Midian would be delivered into his hand, but now Gideon was hearing these words from the mouth of his enemies as well. They were confirming the promise of God's word. The promise of victory on Gideon's behalf.

It was no coincidence that Gideon would just so happen to sneak up on the host of Midian and overhear this random conversation about the dream and its interpretation. God told Gideon exactly what to do, where to go, and who to take. It all happened by divine appointment. God intended to give him another sign to reassure him of the victory he was hoping for.

What more could somebody possibly need to be encouraged? Even the enemy was able to recognize and confess that God had delivered their army into the hands of Gideon.

This is what finally motivated Gideon to become the leader he was meant to be. The Lord did all these things to increase the faith of Gideon. He knew that the investment He put into this man would eventually pay off.

God knows exactly who He can invest in. He knows exactly who will respond to the upward calling. He knows who will heed the signs and wonders. He knows who He can trust with responsibility. He knows everything. He ultimately knows who is going to make it into the kingdom of heaven and who isn't. That is why He gives signs to some while others will only get the sign of Jonah. That is why some hearts he softens and others he hardens. It's because He already knows how we are going to respond to Him.

The Lord also knew that Gideon would worship Him in the beauty of Holiness after the signs were given. That is exactly what Gideon did. He saw that the victory was already his and he worshipped God.

And he divided the three hundred men into three companies, and he put a trumpet in every man's hand, with empty pitchers, and lamps within the pitchers. Judges 7:16

Gideon's army of 300 was divided into 3 groups. The number 300 is jointly connected to the number 3 which is significant in purpose and visible throughout scripture.

Symbolically we cannot look at the number 3 without considering the Holy Trinity. The word trinity is not mentioned in the Bible but it is a logical concept. The Father, the Son, and the Holy Spirit are one. One God, three distinct manifestations. 1 in essence 3 in person.

The number three represents the trinity. Gideon's army was reduced to 300 so that the soldiers could not take credit for the victory God was about to give. Therefore, we know that the number in this scripture represents the strength of God. It represents His omnipotence. If you divide the infinite power of God into three parts you will find that each part will still have the same infinite power. Infinity divided by any number is still infinity. This means that each member of the trinity has infinite power.

When Gideon divided the men into 3 groups he was using

a God given strategy for his attack. Each group would bear the infinite power of God. The omnipotence, the omnipresence, and the omniscience of God would rest on all three groups individually.

Gideon was using the wisdom of God as he planned his attack on Midian. His soldiers would come in from 3 different directions so that the enemy would think they were being surrounded. Hearing the sound of 300 trumpets would lead the enemy to believe that 300 crowds were coming in for the attack.

The trumpets, the lamps and pitcher also had a significant purpose and meaning. These were the weapons of their warfare. These are the weapons that would be used for the pulling down of strongholds.

And he said unto them, Look on me, and do likewise: and, behold, when I come to the outside of the camp, it shall be that, as I do, so shall ye do. Judges 7:17

Gideon was about to set an example for the rest of the soldiers to follow. He said "watch me and do as I do." This verse goes hand in hand with 1 Corinthians 11:1 where the apostle Paul said "follow me as I follow Christ."

As a leader you can set a Christ-like example for others to follow. A leader knows first how to follow and take orders before he gets placed at the front of the crowd.

Follow me as I follow Christ means that we first follow the perfect example of our Lord Jesus Christ before we can lead anyone anywhere. We allow Him to give us the influence and inspiration to be fishers of men.

A good leader will be the first one on the battlefield and the last to leave. A good leader will raise up other leaders. If you are a good leader, people will follow you into leadership.

There are people everywhere who need someone to lead them on the path of righteousness. Someone who can set a perfect Christ-like example. Someone who is willing to lay their life down for the cause. Someone who will stay committed without compromising.

Gideon was that man who was willing to set the example for others to follow. Perhaps God has called you to do the same.

When I blow with a trumpet, I and all that are with me, then blow ye the trumpets also on every side of all the camp, and say, The sword of the Lord, and of Gideon. So Gideon, and the hundred men that were with him, came unto the outside of the camp in the beginning of the middle watch; and they had but newly set the watch: and they blew the trumpets, and brake the pitchers that were in their hands. And the three companies blew the trumpets, and brake the pitchers, and held the lamps in their left hands, and the trumpets in their right hands to blow withal: and they cried, The sword of the Lord, and of Gideon. Judges 7:18

Keep in mind that Gideon's army was divided into three companies. At the beginning of middle watch Gideon, and the hundred men that were with him sounded the trumpets. This would signal the other two companies who were on the sides of the camp to do the same.

All 300 men had torches inside of their pitchers. This gave them the ability to sneak up on the enemy unnoticed. When the trumpets were blown from all 3 crowds the pitchers were broken and the torches were burning brightly. All the noise from the trumpets along with the sudden burst of light on every side would startle the enemy.

The enemy would be even more terrified when all 300 men cried out on one accord, "The sword of the Lord and The sword of Gideon!" They would be particularly fearful because of the dream that the Midianite soldier had about the cake of barley bread tumbling into their camp, and the interpretation thereof.

All who had heard about the dream would panic when they heard the sword of the Lord and the name of Gideon being shouted out loud. They would recognize that the fulfillment of the prophetic dream was coming to pass.

Sounding the trumpets was not only a call to battle, it was also a declaration of victory. The trumpets were made of rams horns which represent salvation. Jesus is the horn of our salvation. The horn was a reminder of God's presence and the help that He provided in times of need.

The pitchers were earthen vessels that were normally used to hold liquids. They represent the flesh of man. We know that they were clay jars because they were easy to break. Just like the clay that's on the potter's wheel: "But we have this treasure in earthen vessels, that the excellency of the power may be of God, and not of us" (2 Corinthians 4:7.)

God chose to use something so fragile and vulnerable to put His power and Glory on display. Men and women are considered to be vessels. The treasure that we have in these earthen vessels is the Holy Spirit.

In verse 16 we find that the lamps were placed inside of the earthen vessels. These lamps were basically lit torches. The fire thereof represents the Holy Spirit and it was placed inside the vessels to declare the work that was going on in the inside of these men. The Holy Spirit was working on the inside. He was cleansing, healing, and strengthening.

When the power of God begins to stir inside of His people it's like a fire that is shut up in our bones. This is Holy Ghost fire. The fire also produces light. "This little light of mine, I'm gon let it shine, let it shine, let it shine."

In order for the light of the lamp to shine the pitcher had to be broken. When the flesh is suppressed the anointing and the power of God is released. The limited strength (weakness) of the flesh has to be crushed in order for God to show His power. The will of the flesh has to be broken so that the will of the Spirit can become more dominant in our lives.

This was the battle for Gideon and his people. It was a battle against the flesh. Against their sins, and the works of the flesh.

Breaking the pitcher has everything to do with breaking the bad habits and putting fleshly appetites into subjection. It is the work that God is doing inside of us that gives us the ability to put our flesh into subjection: "Not by might, nor by power, but by My Spirit saith the Lord" (Zechariah 4:6).

Once the will of our flesh is broken the light within us will shine bright. When the light begins to shine the darkness will flee from it. As we put to death the deeds of the flesh people will begin to see the fire and the light inside of us. The world doesn't need to see us, they need to see the God inside of us.

The sword of the Lord and of Gideon was shouted out loud by all 300 soldiers as part of the strategy. It was done so that the host of Midian would recall the dream and the interpretation thereof and panic.

The 300 soldiers were careful to put the name of the Lord first. Their loyalty was to the Lord. Yet as servants of the Lord we will find that loyalty to God is also loyalty to the man of God.

The soldiers were also showing loyalty to Gideon because he was a manifestation of God's work at that time. They saw his dedication. They saw his life on the line. They saw that he was all in, ten toes down, and they honored him just like we should honor our pastors and leaders in the church.

They knew it wasn't about Gideon. It was about the Lord. The sword of the Lord and of Gideon is the Word of the Lord being entrusted to Gideon for the purpose of execution.

God told Gideon that he would gain victory over the Midianites with only three hundred soldiers. Gideon took God's word as the truth and declared it to his soldiers. His soldiers also believed it as the truth and declared it as well.

The Word of God is not meant to be debated, it is meant to be declared. Declaring the truth is a strategy that we all use to this day. We take the Word that God entrusts us with and we declare it by faith. Every commandment, every prophecy, every warning, and every promise that God gives us we believe and we declare.

And they stood every man in his place round about the camp; and all the host ran, and cried, and fled. And the three hundred blew the trumpets, and the Lord set every man's sword against his fellow, even throughout all the host: and the host fled to Bethshittah in Zererath, and to the border of Abelmeholah, unto Tabbath. Judges 7:21-22

When the light shines the darkness will flee. As the torches blazed the host of Midian fled. Gideon's army stood their ground and sounded the trumpets again. At this point the Lord set all the host against one another. Perhaps they all began to suspect treachery from one another. After all, they were an alliance that consisted of different nations. It could be, that while they fled into the darkness, they could not tell the difference between their allies and enemies.

With the unexpected sound of the trumpet and the sudden blaze of torches they were thrown into a state of terror and confusion. With swords drawn they began to slay each other.

In all reality it was the Lord who was working behind the scenes. It was the Lord who put the enemy in a state of terror and caused them to point their weapons at one another. It was the Lord who was setting the victory in place. And although He could have annihilated the enemies completely, He allowed some of the enemies to make it out of the valley alive.

Those that were still alive after the slaughter fled to Bethshittah in Zererath, and to the border of Abelmeholah, unto Tabbath.

And the men of Israel gathered themselves together out of Naphtali, and out of Asher, and out of all Manasseh, and pursued after the Midianites. And Gideon sent messengers throughout all mount Ephraim, saying, come down against the Midianites, and take before them the waters unto Bethbarah and Jordan. Then all the men of Ephraim gathered themselves together, and took the waters unto Bethbarah and Jordan.

And they took two princes of the Midianites, Oreb and Zeeb; and they slew Oreb upon the rock Oreb, and Zeeb they slew at the winepress of Zeeb, and pursued Midian, and brought the heads of Oreb and Zeeb to Gideon on the other side Jordan. Judges 7:23-25

Naphtali, Asher, and Manasseh were particularly mentioned as the tribes that gathered themselves together to pursue the enemy. These were the same people who were fearful. These were also the same ones who bowed their knees to drink. The same ones who were sent home in the first place. It could be that they tarried in the distance long enough to see the enemy flee and now decided to join the pursuit.

Gideon also sent messengers throughout all of Mount Ephraim, so that the men thereof would also come down against Midian. Ephraim took the waters unto Bethbarah and Jordan and slayed the two chief commanders.

It wasn't until God scattered His enemies, showed His power, and got His glory that the other tribes were able to get involved. At this point the they were ready and willing to be fellow-laborers in the work of God.

And the men of Ephraim said unto him, Why hast thou served us thus, that thou calledst us not, when thou wentest to fight with the Midianites? And they did chide with him sharply. Judges 8:1

The men of Ephraim were displeased with Gideon. They came at him with anger and scolded him sharply because he neglected to invite them to the initial battle.

They were not satisfied with being part of the latter end. They were not satisfied with the role they played. They lent a helping hand to Gideon, and they were a part of God's master plan, but they wanted more. Therefore we come to the conclusion that what they really wanted was the glory as well.

They knew that Gideon would be remembered as a hero and they envied his spotlight. They wanted it for themselves. They wanted to boast about how they brought deliverance to the people.

This is why God reduced the crowd in the first place. He knew the condition of their hearts. Ephraim came into the battle seeking recognition. Otherwise they would have been satisfied with the part they played.

In Judges 12:1 we will find Ephraim doing the same thing with

Jephthah. They were angry when Jephthah went out to war without them.

These were men of proud spirits. They had the wrong motives. They got offended because things didn't go their way.

It's important that we do not approach ministry with this attitude. We are not in this for recognition. We are not seeking a spotlight. We seek to glorify God.

We all have a role to play. Every role is different but every role is important. Just be thankful that we are all a part of God's master plan.

And he said unto them, What have I done now in comparison of you? Is not the gleaning of the grapes of Ephraim better than the vintage of Abiezer? God hath delivered into your hands the princes of Midian, Oreb and Zeeb: and what was I able to do in comparison of you? Then their anger was abated toward him, when he had said that. Judges 8:2-3

Instead of explaining to Ephraim that it was the Lord's decision to start this battle without them, Gideon uses a different biblical approach. He responded with humility. He used a soft answer to turn away wrath (Proverbs 15:1).

He starts by saying that the leftovers of Ephraim (gleaning of grapes) were better than the whole grape harvest of Abiezer (vintage). In other words he said; "what you guys accomplished at the end of this battle was far greater than we did throughout the whole thing. Oreb and Zeeb were delivered into your hand. You guys took out the princes of Midian."

He gave them the praise that they were looking for and with these words the resentment of Ephraim subsided. This confirms the fact that Ephraim was looking for recognition. They got what they wanted and their anger decreased.

And Gideon came to Jordan, and passed over, he, and the three hundred men that were with him, faint, yet pursuing them. Judges 8:4

Although Gideon and his men were exhausted by the time they crossed the Jordan river they still pursued their enemy. They had been in this pursuit for a long distance and they were ready to faint yet they continued. All those who fight the good fight will reach this point at one time or another. Faint, yet pursuing.

It is true that every Christian will be successful in their struggles but we will struggle nonetheless. There will be times when we get exhausted in our battle against sin. We will get tired we will feel like we can't go on but we learn to rely solely upon the perfect strength of God to persevere: "But those who trust in the LORD will find new strength. They will soar high on wings like eagles. They will run and not grow weary. They will walk and not faint" (Isaiah 40:31 NIV).

And he said unto the men of Succoth, Give, I pray you, loaves of bread unto the people that follow me; for they be faint, and I am pursuing after Zebah and Zalmunna, kings of Midian. And the princes of Succoth said, Are the hands of Zebah and Zalmunna now in thine hand, that we should give bread unto thine army? And Gideon said, Therefore when the Lord hath delivered Zebah and Zalmunna into mine hand, then I will tear your flesh with the thorns of the wilderness and with briers. Judges 8:5-7

Gideon knew that his soldiers were just as exhausted as he was. Out of compassion for them, he decided to ask the inhabitants of Succoth for loaves of bread to feed his men. The men of Succoth were also Israelites yet they refused to help out. They refused to lend a helping hand.

They were not asked to engage in the battle itself. They were only asked to feed and refresh the soldiers who fought on the front line.

Their refusal was due to the fact that Zebah and Zalmunna had not yet been delivered into Gideon's hand. This goes to show how fearful the men Succoth were. They feared that if they fed these soldiers, and they did not win, then it would backfire on them.

Gideon on the other hand was confident of the victory. He said "when (not if) the Lord hath delivered Zebah and Zalmunna, that he would tear their flesh with the thorns of the wilderness and with briers."

As you can see, Gideon had developed such a great faith but his love towards difficult people needed work. Love is patient and he was not too patient with the people of Succoth. He was easily angered as you could see that his response towards them was nothing like the soft answer that dwindled the wrath of Ephraim. His response towards Succoth was not so Godly in any way. He made threats.

These people did not help Gideon but they were still God's people. Succoth was Israel's first camp out of Egypt inhabited by the tribe of Gad. They were brethren. Keep in mind that we do not wrestle against flesh and blood but against principalities, against powers, against the rulers of the darkness of this world, against spiritual wickedness in high places.

This is what Midian represents. They are symbolic to the sin, whereas the men of Succoth represent the sinner. As Christians we are taught to love the sinner and hate the sin. We have to learn to respond properly when the sinner treats us wrongly. We have to be patient with those that should be helping out but put up resistance instead. We cannot let them hinder nor discourage our work in the Lord.

And he went up thence to Penuel, and spake unto them likewise: and the men of Penuel answered him as the men of Succoth had answered him. And he spake also unto the men of Penuel, saying, When I come again in peace, I will break down this tower. Judges 8: 8-9

The men of Penuel were also Israelites and they refused to give bread to Gideon as well. This was the sin of Succoth and Penuel. They knew to do well and they did not do it (James 4:17). Therefore, Gideon vowed to break down the tower in their city which was more than likely their confidence and security. Gideon vowed to take vengeance on Succoth and Penuel.

The Bible tells us that vengeance is the Lord's (Deuteronomy 32:35). We should never take vengeance into our own hands. Instead, we must leave room for God's wrath. Not only does Gideon make threats of vengeance but he later follows through.

Now Zebah and Zalmunna were in Karkor, and their hosts with them, about fifteen thousand men, all that were left of all the hosts of the children of the east: for there fell an hundred and twenty thousand men that drew sword. And Gideon went up by the way of them that dwelt in tents on the east of Nobah and Jogbehah, and smote the host; for the host was secure. And when Zebah and Zalmunna fled, he pursued after them, and took the two kings of Midian, Zebah and Zalmunna, and discomfited all the host. And Gideon the son of Joash returned from battle before the sun was up, Judges 8:10-13

Gideon and his 300 persevered until they conquered the enemy. They traveled all the way to Karkor which is unknown territory east of Nobah and Jogbehah. 120,000 enemy soldiers had already fallen in the initial battle and only 15,000 of them were left standing. The enemy was also exhausted from the pursuit and as they reached their territory they settled in to rest.

They thought they had gotten away. They thought their territory was secure but Gideon fell upon them unawares and smote the whole camp taking the two kings prisoner. He had returned from battle victoriously before the sun even touched the sky.

And caught a young man of the men of Succoth, and enquired of him: and he described unto him the princes of Succoth, and the elders thereof, even threescore and seventeen men. Judges 8:14

On his way back from Karkor, Gideon stopped in Succoth to take care of some unfinished business with those who denied him help. He laid hold of a young man in the city to get some information about the rulers thereof. The rulers were the ones responsible for denying Gideon and his men the help that was needed. The young man gave a description of seventy- seven men in total.

With this many rulers in the city we are led to believe that Succoth was a place of great importance. The names, the description, and the dwelling of these great men were probably written so that Gideon would be able to identify and remember each man without bringing harm to anybody else. His intentions were only to bring punishment to those who made the decision to deny him help him in the first place.

And he came unto the men of Succoth, and said, Behold Zebah and Zalmunna, with whom ye did upbraid me, saying, Are the hands of Zebah and Zalmunna now in thine hand, that we should give bread unto thy men that are weary? And he took the elders of the city, and thorns of the wilderness and briers, and with them he taught the men of Succoth. And he beat down the tower of Penuel, and slew the men of the city. Judges 8:15-17

Gideon approached the rulers of the city with Zebah and Zalmunna in plain view. He wanted the men of Succoth to see with their own eyes that he had captured the men whom they doubted he would defeat. They were now in his hands as prisoners of war.

It is obvious that Gideon left Zebah and Zalmunna alive for this very reason. They should have been slain on sight and on arrival. Instead, Gideon took them as prisoners to present them before the rulers of Succoth.

He goes on to remind them of how they denied him help when he and his men were in pursuit of them. Then he took the rulers of that city and taught them a lesson using thorns and briers. He also beat down the tower of Penuel just as he had vowed and slayed the men of that city as well.

Gideon took vengeance on Succoth and Penuel for how they treated him and his men. Although both cities were treacherous and selfish in their actions, they were still part of God's chosen nation. They were Israelites.

Gideon was called by the Lord to deliver Israel from bondage, not to bring them harm. By taking vengeance into his own hands, Gideon was setting a bad example in his leadership. He was misrepresenting the Lord. The Bible clearly states that you shouldn't even say that you are going repay evil to any man according to his works.(Proverbs 24:29). The Bible also teaches us that vengeance belongs to God (Deuteronomy 32:35).

Keep in mind that this is Old Testament scripture as well. Even the scripture that said an eye for an eye was taken out of context.

It was not a personal law, it was a national law. It wasn't something that people were supposed to do on their own. It was something that was supposed to be handled with the help of the civil court system. They are the ones that have the right to exact justice when a crime is committed.

An eye for an eye was not meant to encourage vengeance, it was meant to limit vengeance. Vengeance is never satisfied with justice. It wants more than justice. It wants to give you more than you deserve. Vengeance wants two eyes for the one that was lost. It wants a whole mouth full of teeth for the one that was knocked out. That is the way human nature expresses itself through vengeance. Therefore the law was made to limit the expression of human nature through vengeance. A life for a life, eye for eye, tooth for a tooth, this was the law of exact retribution.

As you can see Gideon was repaying the people of Succoth and Penuel with far more than they deserved. He slayed the men who didn't support him. That wasn't an exact retribution. That wasn't portraying Godly character. Therefore we know that Gideon was on his own agenda during this point in time.

Keep in mind that God is love. He always has been and He always will be a God of love. He is the same yesterday, today, and forever. Even in Old Testament times, God has always been about love and forgiveness. Love is the fulfillment of God's law. We love because He first loved us. After experiencing His love upon our own lives we should be more than willing to share it with others. We are to love others with the same love with which He loves us.

The love of God is patient. He demonstrated His love for us by sending Christ to die for us while we were still sinners.

Gideon was not demonstrating that kind of love toward the people of Israel. Instead he was holding record of their wrong.

The Bible teaches us to love our enemies. Love is greater than faith and hope. Faith pleases God (Hebrews 11:6) and hope gives us perseverance (Isaiah 40:31) but love covers a multitude of sins (1 Peter 4:8). Although Gideon had faith to move mountains and hope that kept him from fainting as he ran his race he still lacked in the area of love.

After taking vengeance upon Succoth and Penuel, Gideon was ready to deal with Zebah and Zalmunna. Apparently, the Midianite kings had killed some men during a battle in Tabor that we do not know much about. The details are not given to us in scripture. We do know that Gideon was trying to find out who was killed in the battle. Gideon must have heard that men were slain in Tabor and suspected them to be his brothers.

Then said he unto Zebah and Zalmunna, What manner of men were they whom ye slew at Tabor? And they answered, As thou art, so were they; each one resembled the children of a king. And he said, They were my brethren, even the sons of my mother: as the Lord liveth, if ye had saved them alive, I would not slay you. Judges 8:18-19

Keep in mind that all of God's children bear the resemblance of a prince. Our Heavenly Father is the King of kings and we resemble Him through the character that we portray.

In this particular verse these words "children of a king" were spoken from a literal standpoint. These were Gideon's blood relatives who had been killed in Tabor. They were the sons of his mother. It is from this very scripture that we can come to a conclusion about Gideon's physical appearance. It's obvious that he had a commanding presence in order to resemble a king. He must've been tall and maybe even fair looking. His brothers had the same resemblance.

Gideon goes on to swear (as the Lord lives) that if his brothers were still alive, he would not slay Zebah and Zalmunna. Keep in mind that God commanded Gideon to destroy these guys (Judges 7:9) and yet the only reason he was going to do it was for personal reasons. Gideon was still on his own agenda acting upon his own motives to destroy the Midianite kings.

Once again, we know that these kings represent the sin of the people. Many times people will utterly destroy certain sin from their lives because it has taken the life of a loved one. For instance, many who have lost brothers, sisters, or parents to drug addiction will grow to hate the drug. They vow never to touch it. They cast it away from their lives not wanting anything to do with it. They utterly destroy it because of the damage it has done to their brethren.

It is ok to want to destroy the sin that has destroyed your family. Yet we must remember that if God tells us to utterly destroy any kind of sin we must be obedient to Him regardless.

And he said unto Jether his firstborn, Up, and slay them. But the youth drew not his sword: for he feared, because he was yet a youth. Then Zebah and Zalmunna said, Rise thou, and fall upon us: for as the man is, so is his strength. And Gideon arose, and slew Zebah and Zalmunna, and took away the ornaments that were on their camels' necks. Judges 8: 20-21

When Gideon ordered Jether to get up and slay the enemies of Israel, he may have been looking to place honor on his son. Gideon's intentions could also have been to train his firstborn to be bold and fearless against the enemies of God.

It wasn't out of disobedience that Jether did not draw his sword, it was out of fear that he refused to obey his father's voice. The Midianite kings were bound but they still managed to intimidate the boy. Jether was just a youth. This is what Zebah and Zalmunna were referring to when they said "as the man is so is his strength." He was young and full of fear. He was not yet in his prime. It would be more humiliating if this youth had the honors of slaying them. Therefore they told Gideon to rise up and do the honors himself. He did, and he also walked away with ornaments that were on their camels' necks. These were the spoils of war.

Then the men of Israel said unto Gideon, Rule thou over us, both thou, and thy son, and thy son's son also: for thou hast delivered us from the hand of Midian. Judges 8:22

Gideon was a man who conquered fear and unbelief. He grew to become a man of great faith. He did some remarkable things through the help of God and therefore the people of Israel wanted him to rule over them. They wanted to crown him as their king and give him a hereditary throne so that his son, and his son's son would rule after him.

Israel failed to recognize God as their king. They decided to be like all the surrounding countries and place man on the throne. Instead of encouraging Gideon in the work of God they gave him credit for the work of God. They said "thou hast delivered us from the hand of Midian." The praise should have been given to God because He was the one who truly delivered them from the hand of Midian. Gideon was just a vessel God used to accomplish His work. Israel failed to see the greatness of God working through Gideon to bring them deliverance. They were so carnally minded that they saw Gideon as the great one. They thought he was the one who brought deliverance with his own strength.

We must always be prepared to direct the praise towards God. Especially when people give us credit for what He has done. The praise of other people can cause man to fall into the temptation of pride and conceit. Pride comes before the fall. If God does a miracle by our hand or uses us to speak a powerful message, we must be ready to give glory where glory is due. It all belongs to God.

And Gideon said unto them, I will not rule over you, neither shall my son rule over you: the Lord shall rule over you. Judges 8:23

Gideon responded properly to the request of kingship. He refuses the position and points the people of Israel towards God. This is what any great leader would do. We have to recognize the sovereignty of the Lord and understand that he alone is king. He is the one who rules on heaven and earth. He is the reason why we have come this far in life. He is the reason why we have conquered addictions and have gotten promotions. He is the reason why we have grown in wisdom and in maturity. He is the reason why we have power over the enemy. The glory belongs to God.

Although Gideon verbally denied the position to rule, his actions in the following verses show he wanted the lifestyle of a king.

And Gideon said unto them, I would desire a request of you, that ye would give me every man the earrings of his prey. (For they had golden earrings, because they were Ishmaelite's.) And they answered, We will willingly give them. And they spread a garment, and did cast therein every man the earrings of his prey. And the weight of the golden earrings that he requested was a thousand and seven hundred shekels of gold; beside ornaments, and collars, and purple raiment that was on the kings of Midian, and beside the chains that were about their camels' necks. And Gideon made an ephod thereof, and put it in his city, even in Ophrah: and all Israel went thither a whoring after it: which thing became a snare unto Gideon, and to his house. Judges 8:24-27

Gideon said that he would not rule over the people of Israel but his actions show otherwise. The first thing that he does is collect gold from the people. That's usually what a ruler would do.

There was a vast amount of gold earrings that they had accumulated from the enemy. The enemy was very wealthy. They even had camels that were decked out in bling around their necks.

Gideon gathered the gold earrings from each person to make an ephod which became a snare to him and his house. An ephod is a sleeveless garment that was only to be worn by the Levitical priests (Exodus 28:4). Scripture doesn't say that Gideon wore the ephod. It doesn't tell us why he built the ephod, but it does say that he put it in the city of Ophrah.

It must've been on display because the people of Israel went chasing after it. We belong to God as a wife does to her husband. When we start running after other things it's like cheating on Him. Those that lust after gold or nice ornaments like the ephod that Gideon made are guilty of Idolatry.

Gideon was anointed as judge, respected as a hero, but he faltered in his leadership. His choices at the end of his story serve as a warning. Even after doing great things through God there is still a possibility of falling.

Thus Midian was subdued before the Israelites and did not raise its head again. During Gideon's lifetime, the land had peace forty years. And Jerubbaal the son of Joash went and dwelt in his own house. And Gideon had threescore and ten sons of his body begotten: for he had many wives. Judges 8:28-30

Despite Gideon's many mistakes and imperfections God used him in such a powerful way that the Midianites never raised their heads again. They never got the courage nor the strength to come against Israel the way they had in times past. The land had rest for forty years during Gideon's lifespan. He was listed in Hebrews hall of faith for what he did in accordance to God's will. He went from fear to faith.

He was a mighty man of valor but his story ended in a mess. He refused the title of a king but he decided to live like one anyway. He had lots of gold and lots of women. Having more than one wife was adopted on a large scale by rulers. Gideon had so many wives that seventy kids came from his loins. Gideon the son of Joash made it to a good old age before he saw death and once again the cycle repeats itself. The children of Israel turned again, and went chasing after Baalim, and made Baal-berith their god. And they forgot the Lord who had delivered them out of the hands of Midian.

And his concubine that was in Shechem, she also bare him a son, whose name he called Abimelech. Judges 8:31

In the Hebrew language the name Abimelech can be interpreted as "my father, the king." With the name Gideon gave to his child we can see that his heart's desires were truly set on being the king. His desires and his decisions ultimately had an effect on his family line.

In Judges chapter 9 we will find the story of Abimelech. He was a man who was bent on having the crown. He wanted to sit on the throne and rule over the people of Israel.

Gideon was anointed as Judge and his position was not inherited by the offspring. If he was king, then Abimelech would've had a chance at receiving the throne.

In Abimelech's eyes his father was a king. His father had power. He had 300 soldiers that carried out his orders at the drop of a hat.

Abimelech wanted to be that guy. He was probably one that hated to be told what to do. He wanted to be the one barking orders at others so that they would do his bidding.

He must've seen all the women his father had taken to his chambers as well. As a young man he probably wanted to do the same. He wanted to take home all the women he saw to his liking. He wanted multiple wives, and concubines.

Abimelech was one of those who went prostituting after the golden ephod that his father built (Judges 8:27). This is one of the reasons it became a snare to the family. Abimelech saw the glimmering gold and was determined by greed to store up riches on earth. He coveted a luxurious lifestyle.

He must've seen the fame that came with the territory. Gideon built up a reputation for himself when he delivered the people from bondage. He received praise and recognition from others and Abimelech wanted that also.

At the beginning of Judges chapter 9 we find that Abimelech goes to his mother's side of the family in Shechem with a crafty little scheme that would help him obtain the throne. He asks them, "would it be better for them if all Jerubbaal's (Gideon's) children ruled over them or just one?" He goes on to remind them that out of all Gideon's children he was their flesh and blood(v2).

His intentions on speaking with his mother's brethren was to provoke jealousy and get them to side with him. Of course their hearts inclined to follow him because he was family and they would benefit from him becoming ruler.

It could be that Abimelech made promises of what he would do for them if he became king. At that time the people of Shechem had been involved in Baal worship. They must've been reminded of the fact that Gideon had broken down the altars of Baal during his lifetime. So they gave money from the temple of Baal-berith to help Abimelech destroy his the house of Gideon. Seventy pieces of silver were given to him from which he hired vain and light persons to follow him into the murder of his brothers.

Seventy pieces of silver was worth a lot more back then and was apparently the price value for the heads of Gideon's sons. Abimelech made his move by killing all his half-brothers except Jotham who was the only one to have escaped.

All the men of Shechem, and all the house of Millo, gathered together to make Abimelech king(v6). The story of Abimelech gives us an example of a man who did what is right in his own eyes. He was the very first Israelite in scripture to have bore the title king. Yet he was really no king at all. God's word clearly states, without contradiction, that there was no king in Israel in the time of judges.

From the murder of his brothers we can tell that Abimelech's heart was not in the right place. We can see what measures a man will take, through the evil of his own heart, to exalt himself into a position of power. Abimelech was willing to kill his own flesh and blood to obtain the title of king.

God had a plan to repay Abimelech and the men of Shechem for the murder of Gideon's sons. After three years of Abimelech's reign, God sent an evil spirit between him and those that helped him rise to power (his family from Shechem)(v.23).

It could be possible that the men of Shechem were a bit disappointed by the way things turned out while Abimelech was in power. Things must have gotten ugly and dark. It goes to show that when wicked bear rule, the people mourn (Proverbs 29:2). So they plotted a way to overthrow him. They dealt treacherously with him. All this would be anticipated by an evil spirit that God sent.

At this time there was a man named Gaal who brought his clan into the city of Shechem and occupied it(v.26). He was a descendant of Hamor, the founder of Shechem. This means he was related to the people of Shechem. He saw that they were in disagreement with Abimelech and saw it as an opportunity to move in and take the crown. He boasted himself in the presence of Shechem and promised them that if he was in command he would get rid of Abimelech. By doing this he convinced them to put their trust in him(v27). Yet there were still some who were loyal to Abimelech. Sometimes people say things in front of the wrong person.

Zebul was ruler of Shechem underneath Abimelech. One of his commanding officers who saw Gaal as a threat to even his own post. If Gaal overthrew Abimelech this could've mean demotion for

Zebul. Therefore he warned Abimelech of Gaal's plan and offered one of his own(v30-33).

In Gaal's attempt to overthrow Abimelech he was driven out and many people of Shechem got hurt that day(v40). This was God's way of taking vengeance on Shechem for aiding Abimelech in the murder of his brothers.

Abimelech's reign also came to an end when he approached a tower in which a group of people had taken refuge. He fought against it and attempted to set fire to it. At this time the Lord used a woman to drop a millstone on his head. Abimelech didn't want it to be said that a woman killed him so he had one of his soldiers run him through with a sword.

This is how God repaid the wickedness that Abimelech had done to his father by murdering his brothers. And these are the words spoken by Jotham the only brother to have escaped Abimelech.

If ye then have dealt truly and sincerely with Jerubbaal and with his house this day, then rejoice ye in Abimelech, and let him also rejoice in you: But if not, let fire come out from Abimelech, and devour the men of Shechem, and the house of Millo; and let fire come out from the men of Shechem, and from the house of Millo, and devour Abimelech. Judges 9:19-20

Jotham put the situation in God's hands and spoke a prophecy that came true. Jotham was afraid of Abimelech. Scripture says that he fled because of fear.

If Jotham would've gotten involved, by taking vengeance into his own hands, then there would've been no room for God to fix things. Things would've only gotten worse for Jotham just like they did for Gideon. Vengeance is the Lord's.

Brothers and sisters, the message we can get from Abimelech's story is that you should never covet a position of power for any reason. Your promotion comes from the Lord. If you exalt yourself you will be abated, if you humble yourself you will be lifted up.

If your heart is in the right place then God will build you up, and when you are ready He will place you in a position from where you can lead. But do not be like Abimelech. There are many people out there who still act this way because they do not have Jesus in their lives.

Those that do not know the king do what is right in their own eyes. They are willing to take extreme measures even in the workplace just to get promoted. They covet the position. They covet power. They are driven by selfish ambition, greed, and hate. Keep in mind that when a person has hate in their heart they are also guilty of murder (1 John 3:15). This story is still so relevant to the lives of many. Whether they do it literally or not they are still killing their own brothers just to rise to power. Just to get a title, a position, a status. Gossiping and setting snares is not a good way to get promotion: "What causes fights and quarrels among you? Don't they come from your desires that battle within you? You desire but do not have, so you kill. You covet but you cannot get what you want, so you quarrel and fight" (James 4:1-2 NIV).

Abimelech was not used by God because he did not make himself available to God. There was no relationship. He was full of selfish ambition and there was nothing great about his deeds.

Now Jephthah the Gileadite was a mighty man of valor, and he was the son of an harlot: and Gilead begat Jephthah. Judges 11:1

There are three things that we learn about Jephthah as we get introduced to him in this verse. First, we learn that he was a Gileadite. This means he resided in the town of Gilead and it brings us to the conclusion that he was from the tribe of Mannasseh.

Secondly, we learn that he was a mighty man of valor. This means that he was a man of strength, courage, and passion. It also means that he was fearless in the face of danger, and bold enough to put his life on the line in battle.

Jephthah was a mighty man of valor but he was also the son of a harlot. This means that Jephthah was dealt a bad hand in life. His mother was known for prostitution. She had many sexual relationships and Jephthah was a product of her sin.

If Jephthah spent any time with his mother as he grew up he would have witnessed her behavior. Imagine how damaging it would be for a child see his mother bringing different men to the house all the time. Especially when the child knows exactly what the mother is doing.

Most women who live this lifestyle do it in plain view of their children. Even if they enter the room and close the door, there is always the sound of squeaking beds and bumping head boards. The child always knows what is going on and it's a painful thing for any child to go through. Even if Jephthah's mother wasn't in the picture, he would've still suffered from the abandonment. Therefore we know that Jephthah had a rough childhood.

The fact is that there are many women and men who put their children through the same thing today. Some of us have witnessed this kind of thing ourselves. Some of us went through childhood feeling abandoned and heartbroken as our parents did what they did to find pleasure in getting high and chasing idols. These things are the root cause of prostitution.

Jephthah was dealt a bad hand but he made the best of it. Despite his circumstances he was a mighty man of valor. The name Jephthah means "set free." It is a name that was fitting for a man who was raised in the worst kind of environment and set free from the bondage thereof. He was a product of his mother's sin but not a product of his environment. He was set free. No matter how bad the living conditions are we can all be set free by the blood of Jesus.

And Gilead's wife bare him sons; and his wife's sons grew up, and they thrust out Jephthah, and said unto him, Thou shalt not inherit in our father's house; for thou art the son of a strange woman. Judges 11:2

Gilead was the name of Jephthah's father. He was married to a woman who gave birth to Jephthah's half-brothers.

Jephthah's half-brothers treated him differently because he was the son of a strange woman. He did not have the same mother as them but this was not the root cause of the rejection. It was over an inheritance. They rejected, and cast him out because they did not want him to share in the inheritance of their father. They were driven by greed. They told Jephthah that it was on account of his mother being a strange woman but they also mentioned the inheritance.

Apparently, Jephthah's mother was no longer in the picture. She was not an active parent in his life. Jephthah was thrust out from his father's house by his brothers. Imagine the hurt, the pain, and the turmoil Jephthah went through from being in a broken home. Abandoned by his mother and rejected by his brothers. It is hard living a life feeling like nobody loves you. Jephthah must've felt unwanted and unloved as he was cast out into a world full of wickedness.

Then Jephthah fled from his brethren, and dwelt in the land of Tob: and there were gathered vain men to Jephthah, and went out with him. Judges 11:3

After being cast out of his father's house Jephthah fled from his brothers. It wasn't fear that caused him to flee. He was a man of courage. In verse 7 we will find that the elders of the city were the ones who expelled him out of his father's house. There must've been some kind of court ruling from which the elders of the city showed favor to Jephthah's half-brothers. He fled because the elders of the city left him no choice.

You could say that Jephthah fled for other reasons as well. He no longer wanted to be in a place where he was not welcome. He didn't want to be placed beneath consideration. Nor did he want to live his life depending on anybody else. Therefore he fled to the land of Tob to make a way for himself.

Jephthah hit the streets with the same attitude that many of society's outcasts would have today. He just didn't care. Like Abimelech, he gathered vain men unto himself and began his walk with the wicked.

In all reality he was searching for acceptance. If he was the one who gathered these men unto himself then he was more than likely their leader. Nevertheless they would have a bad influence on his behavior as well.

Many people who are called to leadership in the church have

spent many years on the streets leading gangs. Jephthah's life is a perfect picture of that scenario.

Jephthah was using his leadership qualities in the wrong way. He was leading these men into vanity. There are so many people today who are doing the same thing. They are leading others into vanity because it's all they know. If they knew better they would do better.

And it came to pass in process of time, that the children of Ammon made war against Israel. And it was so, that when the children of Ammon made war against Israel, the elders of Gilead went to fetch Jephthah out of the land of Tob: And they said unto Jephthah, Come, and be our captain, that we may fight with the children of Ammon. And Jephthah said unto the elders of Gilead, Did not ye hate me, and expel me out of my father's house? and why are ye come unto me now when ye are in distress? And the elders of Gilead said unto Jephthah, Therefore we turn again to thee now, that thou mayest go with us, and fight against the children of Ammon, and be our head over all the inhabitants of Gilead.
Judges 11:4-8

Notice how the elders of Gilead came to fetch Jephthah when they needed help. These were the same people who expelled him out of his father's house. The ones who rejected him in the first place were now requesting his help.

They went to Jephthah because he was the only one who had the necessary qualities to lead and protect the country in this time of peril. He was a mighty man of valor and he was fit for the task to deliver the people of Israel.

Throughout the history of this world people have treated God the same way. They reject Him and cast Him out of their lives but the moment that trouble comes they run to Him for help. Does that sound familiar? I'm sure we have all been guilty of this behavior at one point or another.

When people find themselves in a jam they realize that the only one who can help is God. He is the only one who is able to deliver, heal, and set us free. After rejecting God, people always come crawling back in the midst of imminent danger.

In like manner, the people of Gilead came crawling back to Jephthah for help. Whether they knew it or not, this man was hand-picked by God to deliver them from their oppression.

And Jephthah said unto the elders of Gilead, If ye bring me home again to fight against the children of Ammon, and the Lord deliver them before me, shall I be your head? Judges 11:9

The elders of Gilead sought Jephthah to lead them in a battle against the Ammonites. They did not come to Jephthah with an apology for how they treated him. They were only there because they wanted him to satisfy their own personal needs. They were in distress. They needed help. They knew that he was a mighty man of valor and they knew that he could lead the people into victory.

Jephthah saw their motives. That is why he asked, "If the Lord delivers the Ammonites into my hand will I still be your head (leader)?" Jephthah was skeptical about trusting the people who rejected him in the first place. He was making sure that if he went out and put his neck on the line, they wouldn't just kick him to the curb again.

He also understood that the victory would come from God alone. It was God who predestined the battle. Jephthah recognized the calling of God upon his life. He knew that it was God calling him to fight this noble fight, not the elders of Gilead. Jephthah heard the call and surrendered to it.

This goes to show that no matter what your past looks like God can use you. It doesn't matter what you've done, or how badly you've been hurt. God still loves you and He still wants to use you.

Jephthah was obedient to the call. This battle was an opportunity to glorify the God who was now at work in his life.

And the elders of Gilead said unto Jephthah, The Lord be witness between us, if we do not so according to thy words. Then Jephthah went with the elders of Gilead, and the people made him head and captain over them: and Jephthah uttered all his words before the Lord in Mizpeh. Judges 11:10-11

Leadership was Jephthah's main concern and it was a condition for his help. Perhaps he wanted to make sure that the people would follow him in the right direction continually. Therefore they made a covenant contract with God as the witness.

At this point Jephthah went with the elders of Gilead and the people of Israel made him captain. As he began to speak all his words in Mizpeh, the presence of God was upon him.

And Jephthah sent messengers unto the king of the children of Ammon, saying, What hast thou to do with me, that thou art come against me to fight in my land? And the king of the children of Ammon answered unto the messengers of Jephthah, Because Israel took away my land, when they came up out of Egypt, from Arnon even unto Jabbok, and unto Jordan: now therefore restore those lands again peaceably. Judges 11:12-13

Before grabbing a sword and spear, Jephthah sent messengers to find out why the Ammonites were making war against Israel. He came to find that they wanted land. They were claiming that Israel took the land from them when they came up out of Egypt. The land that they were referring to was Arnon, even unto Jabbok, and unto the Jordan.

And Jephthah sent messengers again unto the king of the children of Ammon: And said unto him, Thus saith Jephthah, Israel took not away the land of Moab, nor the land of the children of Ammon: But when Israel came up from Egypt, and walked through the wilderness unto the Red sea, and came to Kadesh; Then Israel sent messengers unto the king of Edom, saying, Let me, I pray thee, pass through thy land: but the king of Edom would not hearken thereto. And in like manner they sent unto the king of Moab: but he would not consent: and Israel abode in Kadesh. Then they went along through the wilderness, and compassed the land of Edom, and the land of Moab, and came by the east side of the land of Moab, and pitched on the other side of Arnon, but came not within the border of Moab: for Arnon was the border of Moab. And Israel sent messengers unto Sihon king of the Amorites, the king of Heshbon; and Israel said unto him, Let us pass, we pray thee, through thy land into my place. But Sihon trusted not Israel to pass through his coast: but Sihon gathered all his people together, and pitched in Jahaz, and fought against Israel. And the Lord God of Israel delivered Sihon and all his people into the hand of Israel, and they smote them: so Israel possessed all the land of the Amorites, the inhabitants of that country. And they possessed all the coasts of the Amorites, from Arnon even unto Jabbok, and from the wilderness even unto Jordan. So now the Lord God of Israel hath dispossessed the Amorites from before his people Israel, and shouldest thou possess it? Wilt not thou possess that which Chemosh thy god giveth thee to possess? So whomsoever the Lord our God shall drive out from before us, them will we possess. And now art thou any thing better than Balak the son of Zippor, king of Moab? did he ever strive against Israel, or did he ever fight against them, while Israel dwelt in Heshbon and her towns, and in Aroer and her towns, and in all the cities that be along by the coasts of Arnon, three hundred years? why therefore did ye not recover them within that time? Wherefore I have not sinned against thee, but thou doest me wrong to war against me: the Lord the

Judge be judge this day between the children of Israel and the children of Ammon. Howbeit the king of the children of Ammon hearkened not unto the words of Jephthah which he sent him. Judges 11:14-28

Jephthah knew that the Ammonites were making false claims. He knew that the land never belonged to them in the first place. He knew this because he was spending time in the word of God.

Jephthah responded to the enemy with scripture. He gave a biblical history lesson. He explained that the land which they possessed was taken from the Ammorites not the Ammonites. He also explained that it was given to them by God as their inheritance.

Jephatha knew this portion of scripture well enough to communicate it. He was rightly dividing the word of truth. He was prepared to make a defense for the reason of his hope. He gave a wonderful and accurate understanding of God's word to shut the mouth of a lying enemy.

He basically said, "God gave us this land and you are not taking it from us. You can possess whatever land your god Chemosh has given you but not ours."

Jephthah was trying avoid an all-out war but he would not negotiate for the land. The king of Ammon did not listen to his words. He ignored Jephthah's information and made ready for war.

Then the Spirit of the Lord came upon Jephthah, and he passed over Gilead, and Manasseh, and passed over Mizpeh of Gilead, and from Mizpeh of Gilead he passed over unto the children of Ammon. And Jephthah vowed a vow unto the Lord, and said, If thou shalt without fail deliver the children of Ammon into mine hands, Then it shall be, that whatsoever cometh forth of the doors of my house to meet me, when I return in peace from the children of Ammon, shall surely be the Lord's, and I will offer it up for a burnt offering. Judges 11:29-31

The Spirit of the Lord came upon Jephthah as he began marching from one city to the next.

Apparently, Jephthah did not know that the victory would be his the moment that he put his trust in God. He wanted confirmation. He began seeking to ensure the help of God by making a foolish vow. He promised God that if he got the victory that he would make a burnt offering out of whatever comes from his house when he returned home victorious.

So Jephthah passed over unto the children of Ammon to fight against them; and the LORD delivered them into his hands. And he smote them from Aroer, even till thou come to Minnith, even twenty cities, and unto the plain of the vineyards, with a very great slaughter. Thus the children of Ammon were subdued before the children of Israel. Judges 11:32-33

Despite the dumb vow that Jephthah made, God wanted to bring deliverance to his people. Despite his flaws and mistakes, God chose to use him.

God gave Jephthah the victory over his enemies. He gave him the strength to overcome and the ability to smite the enemy with a such a great slaughter.

In the same way God has given us victory over our enemies as well. The Bible says that we are more than conquerors through Christ who loves us (Romans 8:37). We have overcome by the blood of the Lamb and by the word of our testimony (Revelation 2:11).

We have no reason to make vows to God to secure our victories. The devil is a defeated foe. We have been given authority over all the enemy (Luke 10:19). No matter how big the battle is, we have the victory.

And Jephthah came to Mizpeh unto his house, and, behold, his daughter came out to meet him with timbrels and with dances: and she was his only child; beside her he had neither son nor daughter. Judges 11:34

When Jephthah finally returned home from the battle, his daughter came out to meet him. She came dancing with timbrels. She was excited about the victory that her father had gained over the enemy and she was dancing in celebration.

Jephthah was a hero in the sight of Israel and even more so in his daughter's eyes. She admired and thought so highly of him.

What she didn't know was that Jephthah vowed to offer whatever came out of the doors of his house to meet him as a burnt offering. She just so happened to be the one who came to meet him.

When Jephthah made his vow to God he wasn't expecting it to be his daughter that would come forth to meet him when he returned in victory. Out of all the people in the world it had to be his only child.

And it came to pass, when he saw her, that he rent his clothes, and said, Alas, my daughter! thou hast brought me very low, and thou art one of them that trouble me: for I have opened my mouth unto the LORD, and I cannot go back. And she said unto him, My father, if thou hast opened thy mouth unto the LORD, do to me according to that which hath proceeded out of thy mouth; forasmuch as the LORD hath taken vengeance for thee of thine enemies, even of the children of Ammon. And she said unto her father, Let this thing be done for me: let me alone two months, that I may go up and down upon the mountains, and bewail my virginity, I and my fellows. And he said, Go. And he sent her away for two months: and she went with her companions, and bewailed her virginity upon the mountains. And it came to pass at the end of two months, that she returned unto her father, who did with her according to his vow which he had vowed: and she knew no man. And it was a custom in Israel, that the daughters of Israel went yearly to lament the daughter of Jephthah the Gileadite four days in a year. Judges 11:35-40

Was Jephthah's daughter actually sacrificed or was she dedicated to a life of virginity? Was it a literal burnt offering or a spiritual one? This is one of the most debated scriptures in the Bible.

There are some who believe that Jephthah actually sacrificed his daughter on the altar as a burnt offering. The reason many believe this is because of the way the text was written. When we look at Jephthah's vow to the Lord in verse 31, it sounds as if he intended to make a literal burnt offering.

It is possible that Jephthah had a human sacrifice in mind. Perhaps he was expecting a servant to come out and meet him when he returned. He said "whatever comes out to meet me," whether animal or human he would sacrifice it as a burnt offering.

Truthfully nobody keeps bulls, rams, and goats in their home? No farm animals would have logically approached him from his home when he returned. Maybe a dog, but if he was planning an animal sacrifice he could've just waited for his daughter to get off the way till an animal came through.

Scripture does not say that she dedicated herself to serve in the house of God as a virgin for the rest of her life. In verse 40 it mentions that she was lamented. It would be a little extreme to mourn for a woman who dedicated her life as a virgin to do the service of the Lord. The lack of detail here also shows that the author may have not wanted to dwell on the tragedy too long.

Others believe that the burnt offering was a spiritual one. They believe that Jephthah's daughter was offered up as a living sacrifice in which she would remain a virgin for the rest of her life. This would have ended Jephthah's bloodline. He would've been devastated to know his lineage would cease on account of his foolish vow. We are told that when Jephthah's daughter came back from her 2 month retreat, she had never known a man. The emphasis here is that she remained a virgin. She never knew a man or the joy of being a mother.

The scripture does not say that she was actually placed on the altar and burned. God does not encourage human sacrifice. He condemns it. He will not ask for it and He will not accept it. Leviticus 20:2 enforced a law that if any of the people of Israel or any of the foreigners in the land committed child sacrifice they were to be put to death. Jephthah was not put to death. Many believe that if he committed this abomination he would have been dealt with accordingly. If he would have sacrificed his daughter at the altar and burned her then there would have been a national uproar. These are the arguments from those who say that the sacrifice was spiritual and not a literal one.

Whether the sacrifice was literal or spiritual, it was wrong. Anybody with spiritual discernment would recognize that Jephthah's vow was rash. It was not spiritually inspired.

The Spirit of the Lord may have been upon him as he marched to Ammon but he was leaning on his own understanding when he made the vow. It is possible for someone to operate in the flesh even though they are filled with the Holy Spirit and empowered by it. Jephthah was operating in the flesh as he made the vow. That just goes to show his human nature. Sometimes we have a tendency to unintentionally let the flesh get in the way of God's work.

Many people wonder why God would still give Jephthah the

victory after making such a rash vow. It is because God is willing to use imperfect people for the sole purpose of blessing others. Despite all of our imperfections, God is willing to use us in the same way.

Perhaps Jephthah's main concern was Deuteronomy 23:21 (When you make a vow to the LORD your God, you shall not delay to pay it; for the LORD your God will surely require it of you, and it would be sin to you.) He made a vow and he intended to keep it. The only problem is that if this vow was a literal offering then it was unlawful. It was wrong.

God does not expect us to keep a promise when we are bound to committing further sin. In Leviticus 5:4-6 there is a law that deals this type of issue (Or if anyone thoughtlessly takes an oath to do anything, whether good or evil (in any matter one might carelessly swear about) even though they are unaware of it, but then they learn of it and realize their guilt— when anyone becomes aware that they are guilty in any of these matters, they must confess in what way they have sinned. As a penalty for the sin they have committed, they must bring to the LORD a female lamb or goat from the flock as a sin offering ; and the priest shall make atonement for them for their sin NIV.)

This scripture tells us that if we made an unlawful vow or an oath that is impossible to fulfill then there is a way out. When we realize our guilt for making a thoughtless promise or negotiation before God then we would have to bring before the Lord sin offering. Nowadays we have the blood of Jesus to cover that.

If it has been revealed to us that the vow is unlawful and we know the guilt thereof then we must confess our sin and turn from it. Jephthah could have made a sin offering instead of sacrificing his daughter. He was knowledgeable about the history of the Bible but he lacked understanding about proper worship.

23

And the men of Ephraim gathered themselves together, and went northward, and said unto Jephthah, Wherefore passedst thou over to fight against the children of Ammon, and didst not call us to go with thee? we will burn thine house upon thee with fire. Judges 12:1

The Ephraimites brought the same argument to Jephthah that they previously had with Gideon. The only difference is that now they were making threats to burn down Jephthah's house. This conflict was rooted in pride and jealousy. Those who are proud in heart will stir up strife. When they saw that the work of God was done effectively through Jephthah, they became angry.

They couldn't stand to see Jephthah nor the people of Gilead getting any kind of recognition above their own. They felt as if they should be regarded with superiority and they felt robbed of an opportunity to receive praise. They were offended because Jephthah was recognized as a great leader.

The childish behavior they portrayed at this time brought light to the character flaws that were developed within them. They should have dealt with their jealousy and pride the moment it surfaced in their quarrel with Gideon. They didn't, and this is what happens when people do not address these kinds of issues.

The more they allowed the jealousy and pride to grow, the more destructive they became to themselves and also to others. Instead of just bringing a heated argument to Jephthah they brought threats to burn his house with fire.

And Jephthah said unto them, I and my people were at great strife with the children of Ammon; and when I called you, ye delivered me not out of their hands. And when I saw that ye delivered me not, I put my life in my hands, and passed over against the children of Ammon, and the Lord delivered them into my hand: wherefore then are ye come up unto me this day, to fight against me? Judges 12:2-3

The Ephraimites claimed that they were not invited to the battle but Jephthah said otherwise. He made sure to mention that he called on them for help. He pointed out the fact that when he called on them they did not show up.

They didn't want to get involved in the dirty work. They were slothful and they were also afraid. Their hands were slack in times of need and they were not concerned about the condition of God's people. They didn't want to fight the battle but when the victory came they wanted to receive the glory.

Jephthah made sure to mention that the glory belonged to God. Jephthah was able to put his life in his own hands because God strengthened him to do so. Ephraim had no right to approach him with anger. They did not want to help him but God did. Therefore he was in the right to proceed in battle without Ephraim.

Then Jephthah gathered together all the men of Gilead, and fought with Ephraim: and the men of Gilead smote Ephraim, because they said, Ye Gileadites are fugitives of Ephraim among the Ephraimites, and among the Manassites. Judges 12:4

Sometimes an open rebuke is necessary. It is important to confront others in their folly so that they do not continue in it. Learning how to do it properly is the tricky part.

Apparently, Jephthah lost his cool when the Ephraimites called him a fugitive. Instead of just expressing his disapproval on account of their behavior he went a little further. He went to war with Ephraim. He went a little too far by striking them with a firm blow.

Isn't it strange that Jephthah tried to resolve the issue with Ammon peaceably but not with the Ephraimites? The people whom he was called to fight against were the ones he tried to keep the peace with. The people whom he was called to deliver were the ones he went straight to war with.

His response to Ephraim was far different than that of Gideon. He didn't use soft words to turn away their wrath. He did not pet their ego.

Instead he used violence on the people whom God loves. It is true that the lips of fools bring them strife, and their mouths invite a beating (Proverbs 18:6 NIV) but the beating should not come from the people of God. If we have been chosen to lead God's people then we should be setting a good example as leaders.

And the Gileadites took the passages of Jordan before the Ephraimites: and it was so, that when those Ephraimites which were escaped said, Let me go over; that the men of Gilead said unto him, Art thou an Ephraimite? If he said, Nay; Then said they unto him, Say now Shibboleth: and he said Sibboleth: for he could not frame to pronounce it right. Then they took him, and slew him at the passages of Jordan: and there fell at that time of the Ephraimites forty and two thousand. Judges 12:5-6

As you can see, the violence escalated into murder. This was not a good thing. The Gileadites made it to where Ephraim could not escape from them. They blocked the passages of Jordan and killed those who tried to pass over. The Gileadites could not tell the difference between their own people and the people of Ephraim except by their speech. Truthfully, there was no difference. They were all Israelites. They were all God's children. When we look around and see men and women of different color and speech we have to realize that we are all the same in God's eyes. We breathe the same and we bleed the same.

The truth is, we spend far too much time fighting amongst each other. People who fight people are fighting the wrong battles.

The real enemy is at work behind the scenes. We have to be wise enough to know how to fight the unseen foe. In the midst of every confrontation there is an unseen force at work to stir up strife. Jephthah couldn't see it because he was too caught up in the heat of the moment. He led Gilead into a battle that took the lives of 42,000 Ephraimites, and now there was blood on his hands.

And Jephthah judged Israel six years. Then died Jephthah the Gileadite, and was buried in one of the cities of Gilead. Judges 12:7

Jephthah made many mistakes as a Judge. He lacked in many areas of his life but God still chose to use him. He was remembered as a hero and his name was mentioned in Hebrews hall of faith.

Nowadays, many of us lack in a lot of places also but the more we study, the more we pray, the more we grow. Who is to say that Jephthah didn't grow in understanding and maturity as he went on to judge Israel for the last six years of his life. God wasn't done with him until his number was called. We can only hope that Jephthah got it right.

24

And the children of Israel did evil again in the sight of the LORD; and the LORD delivered them into the hand of the Philistines forty years. Judges 13:1

Once again the people of God decided to go back to their sinful ways. They did what they saw fit. They totally disregarded the commandments of the Lord and decided to live according to their own will.

The cycle repeats itself and now we are introduced to another enemy, the Philistines. The children of Israel were under subjection to this enemy for 40 years before God intervenes.

And there was a certain man of Zorah, of the family of the Danites, whose name was Manoah; and his wife was barren, and bare not. And the angel of the LORD appeared unto the woman, and said unto her, Behold now, thou art barren, and bearest not: but thou shalt conceive, and bear a son. Now therefore beware, I pray thee, and drink not wine nor strong drink, and eat not any unclean thing: for, lo, thou shalt conceive, and bear a son; and no razor shall come on his head: for the child shall be a Nazarite unto God from the womb: and he shall begin to deliver Israel out of the hand of the Philistines. Judges 13:2-5

In this verse we find a woman who was given a promise by an angel concerning a child that would be born unto her. The woman was barren but the angel assured her that she would conceive. There was also a promise that the child would begin to deliver Israel out of the hands of the Philistines.

There was a set of instructions linked to these promises. She was instructed not to drink wine nor any strong drink. She was told not to eat anything unclean. It was also mentioned that no razor should come upon his head.

In like manner, God has given us promises along with instructions concerning our own children. The Bible says, "Now choose life, so that you and your children may live" (Deuteronomy 30:19 NIV).

As you can see the promise is not just for us but also for our children. We are instructed to choose life with the promise of our children receiving it as well. To choose life is to choose Jesus. He is the way, the truth, and the life. If we choose Jesus then we may live and our children may live as well.

To choose Jesus is to fully devote our lives to following Him. And abiding by His word without compromise. If we do this with the right heart the scripture says that we shall live and our children will live as well.

What does it mean to live?

It should be noted that someone who truly has life is filled with the Holy Spirit. It is when a person finds their purpose that they truly live. To live is to have purpose. So if God promised that your children will live if you follow instructions then that means your child will find his or her purpose in life. The word live also reaches to eternity.

Also remember that when Noah built the ark it was for the saving of his house. Not just for himself. The Bible said "if you believe in Christ you and your house hold shall be saved" (Acts 16:31).

If you fully obey the Lord and carefully follow all His commands then your child shall be blessed (Deuteronomy 28:1,4). This does not

ADRIAN LOPEZ

mean that your child is going to live a life without struggles and tribulations. This does not mean that your child will have a Rolls Royce and a mansion. According to the Oxford dictionary, to be blessed is to be made holy, consecrated.

According to God's Word, this is what it means to be blessed: Blessed are those whose sins are forgiven (Psalm 32:1), blessed are the pure in heart (Matthew 5:8), blessed are the peace makers (Matthew 5:9), blessed are those who hear the word of God and keep it. (Luke 11:28)

God is promising that your child will be blessed. That means he/she will be made holy and that their sins will be forgiven. That your child will hear the word of God and keep it.

Now keep in mind, if you want to see your child blessed, and living with purpose, you have to obey His word and follow all biblical instructions concerning them.

Our children are to be considered as more than just a responsibility. We are entrusted to raise them in the ways of the Lord. Scripture tells us to train them in the way they should go so that when they are old they will not depart (Proverbs 22:6). It also tells us that if we spare the rod we spoil the child (Proverbs 13:24). We are taught not to provoke them but to bring them up in the discipline and instruction of the Lord (Ephesians 6:4).

We have to be tough as parents and put our trust in God. We must learn to cast all our cares upon Him and cleave to the promises He has given us concerning our children even when things don't look too promising.

As we continue to read the story about the child whom Manoah's wife conceived we will find that he was a little bit stubborn. The promises of God didn't happen exactly the way Manoah's wife would have wanted them to, but they did come to pass nonetheless.

It's insane to think of what children put their parents through. It can be a challenge not to worry over a child who is living wrong but as Christians we have to understand that worrying about anything is sinful. We do not worry about our children because we trust God and we know the promises He has made concerning them. God knows the end from the beginning and if He promises anything concerning our children we can trust that what He said will come to pass.

We know, from the story of Abraham, that the promises of God can take years to fall into place. Even if your child is a grown man and still living wrong, just continue to do your part. Remind God of His promises and declare them in prayer. Stay obedient and keep your faith no matter what the situation looks like. God's timing is better than ours.

And Samson went down to Timnath, and saw a woman in Timnath of the daughters of the Philistines. And he came up, and told his father and his mother, and said, I have seen a woman in Timnath of the daughters of the Philistines: now therefore get her for me to wife. Then his father and his mother said unto him, Is there never a woman among the daughters of thy brethren, or among all my people, that thou goest to take a wife of the uncircumcised Philistines? And Samson said unto his father, Get her for me; for she pleaseth me well. Judges 14:1-3

God had promised Manoah's wife that her son (Samson) would begin to deliver the Israelites out of the hand of the Philistines, yet from the beginning of his adult life we find Samson doing things contrary to what the Lord promised her. I know that there are many parents who can relate to this. God has made some promises about our children, yet we see them doing the exact opposite of what He promises.

Instead of making war with the Philistines, Samson was intermingling with them.

It is not clear what business Samson had going down to Timnath In the first place. It is not clear if his intentions were to find a wife in that area.

It is evident that he was in enemy territory. From the beginning of his story we find him out of place.

Timnath was a Philistine city located in Canaan about four miles from Dan. While he is there he sees a woman who looks pleasing to the eye. "Get her for me," he tells his parents.

In those times it was common for parents to take wives for their sons. The parents of the bridegroom would pay a bride price or a dowry to the parents of the bride. Cattle, property, or cash to ensure that she is properly taken care of and comfortable as she leaves her family to live with her new husband. Perhaps this is why Samson asked his parents to get the woman for him. They would be the ones to do the negotiation.

They were pretty much taken aback. Their response showed that they were in disagreement with Samson but eventually, they gave in.

As parents we all want the best for our children. We want to see them get involved in a good marriage. Find someone in the church who loves God. Someone who will be a suitable help for them.

Samson had a weakness. He saw a woman that looked pleasing to the eye. His judgment was based on her outer appearance but inwardly her heart was not in the right place. She was an uncircumcised Philistine. This means she was not a worshipper of God.

His parents knew that this would be a very dangerous situation. Scripture tells us that the Israelites were not to intermarry with Canaanites (Deuteronomy 7:1-3). The Philistines were a people who lived on the south coast of Canaan. For Samson to take this woman to be a bride he would be breaking God's law.

But his father and his mother knew not that it was of the Lord, that he sought an occasion against the Philistines: for at that time the Philistines had dominion over Israel. Judges 14:4

Samson marrying this pagan woman was of the Lord. God had a strategic plan to bring out His purpose through Samson's mistakes. It is not that God wanted Samson to marry this pagan woman because God does not go against His own will, but before Samson was even born God already knew that he would make this mistake. God already knew how to deal with it and how to bring out His own purpose even through Samson's mistake. God can make all things come together for our good. He can use our mistakes to position us right where He wants us to be.

Samson falling for this uncircumcised Philistine woman was of God because God sought an occasion against the Philistines. Samson was predestined to start delivering Israel out of the hands of the Philistines. God knew how to use that weakness to put Samson right where he was meant to be. In battle.

As we continue the story we will find that God does keep His promise to Manoah's wife. He uses Samson to start delivering Israel out of the hands of the Philistines. He does it in a way that the parents least expected to see it. Nevertheless, God kept His word. God will keep His word concerning our children too.

Let's just hope our children do not have to go through what Samson went through in order to find their way. Samson was a really stubborn man and he was really weak towards his flesh. Yet God still used him and God can still use our children too. No matter what your child is going through at the moment. No matter where he/she is in life you have to keep on trusting and hanging on to the promises of God.

Keep on praying for your children and thank God ahead of time for coming through on their behalf. He already has a strategic plan set in motion for your child. He can bring your children to their knees without breaking free will. He can close doors that no one else can open and open doors for them that no one else can close.

If your child is caught up in any kind of wrong living, God can make His way in. He can make it to where a drug addict will no longer enjoy his high. He can frustrate the works of any gang member, prostitute, or sinner of any kind.

The plan is already set in motion for your child. He created your child. He knows your child inside and out. The thing that upsets you about your child could be the very thing that God is going to use to bring His own purpose through your child. God does work in mysterious ways.

As we look back at our own lives we could see exactly how God uses the very thing that was destroying us to draw us in. In one way or another we were all sick or imprisoned from some kind of sin when we cried out.

The very thing that was destroying us and causing us to do things that we normally wouldn't do, is what He used to bring us to our knees. It was of the Lord. He knew that the addiction would make a mess of us to the point where we would cry out. Although God did not intend for any of us to be hooked on drugs, He knew that some of us would be foolish enough to do them anyways. Therefore, He decided to use the sin as a clutch bring us to Him.

God can make His way into the life of any person no matter how stubborn they are. Just look at the entrance He made into the life of apostle Paul. God has designed all of us including our children in such a way where He can reach us.

Then went Samson down, and his father and his mother, to Timnath, and came to the vineyards of Timnath: and, behold, a young lion roared against him. Judges 14:5

Some people say that Samson was a spoiled little brat because his parents gave in to his request. Although they did not want him to marry this woman they still went down to Timnath to get the woman.

Perhaps they could have said no. Maybe they tried to, but when a grown man's heart is set on pursuing a woman, who can stop him?

Samson was determined to marry this woman. This is the reason from which he and his parents went down to Timnath.

God loves marriage. He designed it so that he can bring two people together in agreement. God said it was not good for man to be alone and therefore provided Adam with a suitable helper. A suitable helper is a woman who will come into agreement with the man to fulfill a God given purpose, vision, or dream. This was God's intentions behind marriage. It is a good thing for a man to find a wife.

One mistake that many Christians make is that they fall for an unsuitable helper. One who doesn't come into agreement with the will of God. One whose focus is carnal, whose words are sweet as honey but in the end are bitter like wormwood. It is important that we wait on God in this area. He has the best in mind for all His children. If He has not withheld His only begotten Son from us but offered Him up for all, then He will freely give us all things.

When God gives, He gives His best. Don't settle for anything less, don't jump into marriage until you know that is what God has for you. When a woman belongs to you, God will bring her to you. You will not have to walk down to Timnath to find her or anyplace else for that matter.

We know that the woman was made from the man. It was a man's rib that God used to create the woman. We also know that the ribs are there to protect many vital organs including the heart. Therefore the woman whom God brings you will be there to protect your heart, not destroy it. She will not hinder you from what God is calling you to do. You will not have to worry about her cheating on you because she will be so focused on pleasing God that she will have no desire to fornicate.

These type of women do exist. These type of men do exist. God has been building up a whole army of men and women who have fled from sexual immorality, fornication, and lust. If you are faithful to Him, then He will send you suitable helper. Just be patient and remember God has the best in mind for you.

Apparently, Samson did not know this. He was a little weak and impatient when it comes to women.

As they enter Timnath in a search for his bride to be we find Samson once again in a place where he had no business being. The vineyard.

Samson was to be a Nazarite from birth. As a Nazarite, Samson had a standard to live by. He could not touch a dead body. He could not shave the hair off his head. He could not drink wine nor touch grapes. Part of the Old Testament Nazarite vow stated that the man of God should separate himself from wine and strong drink. It also stated that he shall not eat moist grapes, nor raisins (Numbers 6:3).

A vineyard is a plantation of grapevines, typically producing grapes used in winemaking. Therefore, Samson should not have been in the vineyard. Whether he was there to find strong drink or just to have a snack he would have been breaking his Nazarite vow.

The scripture does not say that he broke his vow at this point in time but it does say that a young lion roared against him. This verse goes hand in hand with 1 Peter 5:8 ("Be alert and of sober mind. Your enemy the devil prowls around like a roaring lion looking for someone to devour NIV)".

In reality we know that Samson had an encounter with a real lion. But the spiritual message behind this text involves the devil who prowls around like a roaring lion seeking someone whom he may devour.

When Samson entered into the vineyard he was being tempted. This scene is similar to the one in Genesis where the serpent tempted Eve to eat from the tree. Yet in this scripture the devil comes in the form of a lion. We see Samson, we see the forbidden fruit, and we see the young lion.

And the Spirit of the Lord came mightily upon him, and he rent him as he would have rent a kid, and he had nothing in his hand: but he told not his father or his mother what he had done. Judges 14:6

If he would have eaten the fruit it would have indicated a victory on the side of the lion (the devil). If he would have fallen into the temptation and drank some wine he would have not been sober minded and vigilant. Instead he would have been devoured. Temptation can be a very hard thing to overcome. That is why we need the Holy Spirit. We need the power and the self-discipline that the Holy Spirit provides to be able to overcome temptation and trample on the lion. This is a pretty interesting scene.

Although his father and his mother went to Timnath with him they were not with him when he wandered out into the vineyard.

The word rent as it is used in this scripture means tear. Samson tore this lion as if he would have torn a kid. The lion was young but it wasn't a baby. It was not a cub. This lion was big enough to attack and devour a human. The lion was probably in its prime.

Samson would have been pretty tough to have torn this lion like a kid. Yet this was not done by the strength of Samson. Scripture says that the Spirit of the Lord came mightily upon him. This was a demonstration of God's power: "You will tread on the lion and the cobra; you will trample the great lion and the serpent. "Because he loves me," says the LORD, "I will rescue him; I will protect him, for he acknowledges my name" (Psalm 91:13-14 NIV).

The fact that the Spirit of the Lord came heavily upon Samson tells us that Samson had a relationship with God. He set his love upon the Lord. The Spirit of God dwells in those who love Him and are willing to yield to His guidance. If any man does not have the Spirit then he is none of His. Samson was a child of God, born of Spirit. This was not the first time that Samson was moved by the Holy Spirit. The Spirit of the Lord had already began to move him at times in the camp of Dan between Zorah and Eshtaol (Judges 13:25). Therefore we know that Samson was already acquainted with the things of God.

As the Spirit came over him he tore the lion as he would have torn a kid. This is what we call demonstration of God's power. He had nothing in his hands yet he was able to tear up a lion that was anywhere from 330 to 500 pounds of pure muscle. Sharp teeth and claws. That is pretty amazing.

Praise be to God who trains our fingers for battle and our hands for war. When our adversary the devil approaches us we can tear him to pieces with our hands alone. All we have to do is put our hands together in prayer, or lift our hands up in praise and by doing this we can demonstrate God's power over the great lion.

One thing that we should always remember is that God is the most powerful source in the universe. He is Almighty God. The great I Am is on our side. He wants to take up residency in us. If we have such a big God living in our little frames it should show. We should be more confident knowing who is on our side. If God is for us who can be against us.

The message behind this story is that we can do the same thing to the devil that Samson did to that lion. In the midst of temptation we can demonstrate God's power. We can trample on the lion by not eating of the forbidden fruit. We can overcome with the help of God's Spirit by saying no to the things that are tempting and forbidden.

The forbidden fruit could represent fornication, drugs, or anything that the devil wants to use to devour you. Although it may look so good and so tempting, you know it's wrong and therefore you don't partake of it. You don't touch it you don't taste you don't handle. You walk away with nothing in your hands. Instead you lift your hands in praise to the one who empowers you to live victorious.

And he went down, and talked with the woman; and she pleased Samson well. Judges 14:7

Ah, yes. Back to the woman. The very reason why Samson went down to Timnath in the first place.

He finally gets to talk to the woman who he was determined to have. The conversation they had was most likely about marriage.

At this point Samson should have been judging the character of this woman to see if she was a suitable helper. It's always important to test the fruit of anyone who we intend to marry.

Samson was more concerned about the outer appearance of this woman than the inner one. Apparently he thought she was a very pleasant woman.

26

And after a time he returned to take her, and he turned aside to see the carcass of the lion: and, behold, there was a swarm of bees and honey in the carcass of the lion. Judges 14:8

After some time Samson returned to marry the woman from Timnath. It is believed that a year had passed since his fight with the lion. This would make the lion's carcass more of a skeleton which would be a lot more suitable for a swarm of bees to make their hive.

The lions carcass was a place of victory for Samson. When he turned aside to see this carcass he was reminded of what went down the day he fought the lion. The whole scene was on replay within his mind. He was reminded of how the Spirit of God came upon him and helped him to overcome this lion. When Samson returned to the lion's carcass he returned to his place of victory.

It is one thing for a person to experience victory and another thing for a person to maintain it. God wants us to gain victory over self, Satan, and sin but He also wants us to maintain that victory. He wants us to walk in victory and continue living in it.

In order to maintain our victory we have to have the right kind of mindset and the right kind of attitude. How we perform on the outside has a lot to do with how we think on the inside. It has a lot to do with the way we perceive things. Victory comes to those who have a warrior's mentality. We gird up the loins of our minds knowing that the life God has for us is not absent from pain, troubles, nor temptation.

We choose not to dwell on certain things. We choose not to live in self-pity or depression. We have made a choice not to be defeated. Victory is a choice. We choose to be strong and disciplined. We chose to be confident and optimistic. This is the attitude that every one of God's children should have.

At the same time we must recognize that our victory comes from God. We do not gain victory by our own strength. We rely on God.

The lion's carcass was Samson's place of victory. Being that he had to return to it tells us that he was no longer walking in it. Throughout his life, Samson wavered back and forth from victory to defeat.

In this particular verse Samson returned to his place of victory. He returned to a place of confidence and surrender to God. The victory Samson had over the lion was not only the outward demonstration of God's power but it started with the inward state of mind and condition of his heart. The Bible says, "guard your heart because everything you do flows from it" (Proverbs 4:23 NIV). This means if we allow sin into our heart our actions will show. The heart of the victorious man or woman of God has to be well protected and in a state of surrender to the will of God.

For the child of God, victory starts at the altar where we surrender our lives and lay our sin before the Lord. This is the very place where we draw near to Him.

When we finally surrender our lives to Christ, He can use us. When we fully surrender our lives over to God, we will gain victory over the enemy. If we are not fully surrendered, then that means the devil has a foothold and there is no victory.

Either you are for God or you are not. If you surrender to God you will gain victory over all, but if not then that means you are serving self, Satan, and sin. There is no victory outside of surrendering to God's will. When you surrender to God you are allowing Him to do the work He intended to do in your life. You are allowing Him to use you to fight against evil. If you live your life in surrender to His will He will bring out the best in you. He will make a warrior out of you.

God is calling us back to the place of victory. Back to the lion's carcass. Back to the place where we trampled on the devil by overcoming temptation. Back to the place where we had a confident and optimistic mindset. Back to the place where the condition of our hearts was pleasing to Him. Back to the place where we were passionate about serving Him. Back to the place where we truly put our trust in Him and as a result we obeyed His every command.

With every step of obedience we can bruise the head of the serpent with our heel. That is the place of victory. God is calling us back to this place and He wants us to take up permanent residence in it. He wants us to live in victory and maintain it as well.

This does not mean that we will not make mistakes, that we will not struggle, or that we will not have our share of suffering. It means that when we encounter opposition we will be determined to push through.

Even in the midst of adversity we have a peace that surpasses all understanding. We have a joy that gives us strength. We have a God who never leaves us nor forsakes us and because we know this we can walk in confidence. Our victory is secure in Christ Jesus.

Looking back to the scene where Samson tore the lion to pieces, we find that the Spirit of the Lord came heavily upon him. This means that Samson was in the Spirit when he gained this great victory. This means he was in the presence of God when he tore the lion. He was past the outer courts, past the brazen altar, he was in the Holy of Holies. To be in the Spirit is to be in a state of worship. We yield to the guidance of the Holy Spirit and get into constant communication with God. We learn to be prayerful, we study to show ourselves approved, and we meditate on His Word day and night. This is what the Spirit of God leads us to: "If the Spirit of God lives in you, however, you are not in the realm of the flesh but are in the realm of the Spirit, if indeed the Spirit of God lives in you" (Romans 8:9 NIV).

When we look back to the place of our greatest victory, we will see that we were trusting in God. Trust and obedience run hand in hand. The moment when we put our trust in God, we will do exactly what He tells us to do.

Some of us have trusted God enough to get outside of our comfort zone. Some of us have literally walked away from everything we knew and everything we had because that is what God asked us to do. Trusting in God leads to obedience, and obedience puts us in a position to be victorious over all our spiritual enemies. We find victory by placing trust in the Lord and sometimes we find ourselves needing to return to that place of victory.

And after a time he returned to take her, and he turned aside to see the carcass of the lion: and, behold, there was a swarm of bees and honey in the carcass of the lion. Judges14:8

Throughout scripture you will find that honey is considered a good thing. For Samson to find honey in the carcass of the lion tells us that he found something sweet when he returned to his place of victory: "pleasant words are as an honeycomb, sweet to the soul, and health to the bones" (Proverbs 16:24).

What could be more pleasant than the words of the Lord? His words are sweet to the soul. They bring health to the bones. When we are in the presence of the Lord, He will speak words of wisdom, He will teach us about life. His words rejuvenate us. They give us strength to continue in the path we walk in.

And he took thereof in his hands, and went on eating, and came to his father and mother, and he gave them, and they did eat: but he told not them that he had taken the honey out of the carcass of the lion. Judges 14:9

In Genesis 43:11 we find that honey is a good gift, so it is not surprising that Samson shared it with his family. When we receive a word from God we should always be willing to share it as a gift to others. Come back to your place of victory, receive a word from God, get rejuvenated, and then rejuvenate your family.

Scripture says that Samson did not tell his parents about the lion that he tore nor did he tell them where he got the honey. It could've been an act of humility that kept Samson from sounding a horn. Perhaps he decided to keep his victory between him and the Lord.

So his father went down unto the woman: and Samson made there a feast; for so used the young men to do. And it came to pass, when they saw him, that they brought thirty companions to be with him. Judges 14:10-11

Samson's father went down to claim the woman from Timnath as his son's bride. During this time, Samson put together a wedding feast which was an essential part of the marriage ceremony.

When the families saw him putting together this feast, they brought him thirty companions to celebrate with him. These were Philistine men who attended his party mostly to act as spies.

The fact that Samson did not bring any of his own people to this marriage shows that it was very unpopular. His people were not in agreement with it.

And Samson said unto them, I will now put forth a riddle unto you: if ye can certainly declare it me within the seven days of the feast, and find it out, then I will give you thirty sheets and thirty change of garments: Judges 14:12

A riddle can be a question or a statement with a double meaning. It is intentionally phrased so that cleverness is required to find out the answer or meaning to it. It is typically presented as a game. A riddle can also be described as a puzzle to be solved.

Samson had a riddle for the thirty men who came to his wedding feast. He promised to give each one of them a sheet and a change of garments if they were able to solve the riddle. On the other hand, he was sure to mention that if they could not solve the riddle they would each owe him a sheet and a change of garments

But if ye cannot declare it me, then shall ye give me thirty sheets and thirty change of garments. And they said unto him, Put forth thy riddle, that we may hear it. Judges 14:13

Notice that the riddle was brought forth with a bet. There

was a gamble behind it. Samson basically made a bet to his thirty companions that they could not solve the riddle. If he won the bet he would gain a sheet and set of clothing from each one of his companions. If he lost the bet he would have to pay each one of them a sheet and a set of clothing, amounting to thirty pieces each. In reality this was a gamble in its truest form.

In this chapter we are going to see how the enemy uses gambling to stir up strife and cause one to stumble.

There are many people who claim that gambling is not a sin and that it is ok to do. There are even some who preach the Gospel who have said that gambling is ok, but it is important that we rightly divide the word, and allow the Spirit to guide us into all truth. It is the Spirit of God living in us that will tell us that gambling is sinful. That same Spirit has led us to these scriptures and will confirm this message.

It is true that the devil has been using gambling as a tool to sneak his way into the lives of countless people. Many of us have had to be rescued from the despair of a gambling addiction. Therefore we know that it's wrong.

Many of us have spent countless hours at the casinos spending money that didn't belong to us. Wishing upon a star, just hoping to win so that we could get out of debt, but it never happens. All we ever get from it is anger, misery, and more debt. That's exactly what the devil wants for us. He uses gambling as a tool to reel people in. He makes it sound like so much fun but he never tells us about the consequences.

The idea for Samson to place this bet came from the enemy. Satan is like a whisper in the wind. He is the voice behind all sin. He places ideas into people's heads that sound so brilliant. He leads us to believe in an outcome that is totally untrue. That is why we must always be on guard having our minds focused to bring every thought captive and put it into the obedience of Christ.

Before we move any further, here are a couple of verses that can support the argument against gambling.

The Bible tells us to be content with our wages (Luke 3:14). When a person is content with their wages they are in a state of peace with what they have. They are satisfied with the provisions of God. Most people who gamble are not content with what they have. They are driven by want.

The Bible also tells us not to covet (Exodus 20:17). The Lord is my Shepherd, I shall not want. He supplies my every need. If you want more than what God has to offer, then you are coveting. Gambling is an evil that is rooted in the love of money. It is the love of money that has people placing bets hoping for such a win that will buy them a nice house or bring them out of debt.

We should never set our hope on riches that are uncertain. There is truly no strength behind this hope. It is unlike the hope that the Lord offers us. The one who has a future and a hope planned for us is always faithful in keeping his word. When our hope is in God we can have a confident expectation in His promises. When we place our hope in anything other than the promises of God it is sinful and it shows lack of trust in the Lord.

A lot of people who gamble are motivated by greed. It is not fitting for a servant to set his heart on money. We cannot serve two masters.

Everything we see and everything we have belongs to God. He is the owner of it all. From the stars in the sky to the houses we live in. Even our children belong to Him and every penny we have no matter how hard we work for it. It all belongs to God. Our increase comes from Him.

(Titus 1:7 For a bishop must be blameless, as the steward of God; not self-willed, not soon angry, not given to wine, no striker, not given to filthy lucre;) This basically teaches us not to get involved with dirty money, not to be greedy for gain but to be thankful for what God provides and to be good stewards of what He has given us. He wants us to manage our money properly. It wouldn't be too proper to squander our livelihood at casinos.

Gambling is addictive. It is not wise to get involved in it. Many people have become ensnared by it.

God wants us to enjoy what we have and He also wants us to help those in need but we cannot do that when we get caught up in greed. This type of evil makes it hard to enjoy what God has for us.

One thing for sure is that we are in the midst of war and our enemies are relentless. The devil is in association with evil spirits who are constantly trying to find a way to get a foothold in our life. Although they are limited in what they can do, they work around the clock (24/7 shift coverage) to deceive as many as they possibly can. They don't take time off nor go on vacation. This is war. The devil wants our souls and he will go to any measure to get what he wants. He comes to steal, kill, and destroy. Therefore we always have to be on guard against his lies. It is important that we learn to discern the truth from a lie.

We should never stop praying, we should never let our guards down. If the devil is out there working as hard as he does then we should be working harder.

Gambling is an addiction that reaches all ends of the earth. Even behind bars there are people who place bets on everything. Some won't even get on the spade table unless there is a soup or some kind of money on the line. They bet on football games and even on chess games. If there is a way to gamble, they will do it. When they don't have soups they bet the dessert off their dinner tray. If nobody wants to put a dessert on the line they will bet for pushups. There are times when people go without a breakfast tray because they were foolish enough to gamble it off.

Many fights have occurred on the count of making bets in jail and prison. This is one of the most common reasons why people fight behind bars. With that being said, we know that it is of the enemy.

Gambling in the free world is a lot different and a lot more dangerous. There are a people who spend days in the casinos squandering off money that doesn't even belong to them. Some people sit there gambling money that they owe to drug dealers.

Those of us who have been in those shoes know the misery that comes with it. We end up so far in debt while gambling just puts us deeper into a pit of despair. What starts off as a little bit of fun turns out to be a whole lot of bitterness.

From the looks of it, Samson had a gambling problem. He had a problem because he was betting for something he did not have (as we will find out later).

We really do not know exactly why Samson was gambling. We don't know if he was being greedy or if he was doing it for sport. Either way he certainly learned a lesson.

And he said unto them, Out of the eater came forth meat, and out of the strong came forth sweetness. And they could not in three days expound the riddle. Juges14:14

The riddle that Samson brought forth was based on a real life experience. When he said "out of the eater" he was referring to the full-grown lion that attacked him, and when he said "came forth meat" (something to eat) he was speaking of the honey he found in the lion's carcass. When he said "out of the strong came forth sweetness" once again his focus was on the lion and the honey.

Samson must have been intrigued by the events that occurred with the lion and the honey. The lion had come to devour him but got devoured instead.

This riddle would have been impossible for the Philistines to figure out. There was absolutely no way they would get it. Or so he thought.

Samson placed this bet with confidence that his companions would not figure out his riddle. Have you ever done something similar? Being so confident in placing a bet because you thought there was no way you could lose. Maybe you placed a bet on skill instead of luck. Something you were really good at and there was no possible way that you would lose, yet somehow you still end up losing.

And it came to pass on the seventh day, that they said unto Samson's wife, Entice thy husband, that he may declare unto us the riddle, lest we burn thee and thy father's house with fire: have ye called us to take that we have? is it not so? And Samson's wife wept before him, and said, Thou dost but hate me, and lovest me not: thou hast put forth a riddle unto the children of my people, and hast not told it me. And he said unto her, Behold, I have not told it my father nor my mother, and shall I tell it thee? Judges 14:15-16

Samson never told his mother or his father about the fight he had with the lion. As we discussed earlier this could have been done out of humility. Perhaps he did not want to sound the horn and stick his chest out for his accomplishments.

On the other hand we see the riddle could have a lot to do with the reason why he never told anybody about the incident with the lion. Nobody knew what he had done besides the Lord and because of this he was confident enough to make a riddle and place a bet on it.

She wept before him the seven days, while their feast lasted: and it came to pass on the seventh day, that he told her, because she lay sore upon him: and she told the riddle to the children of her people. And the men of the city said unto him on the seventh day before the sun went down, What is sweeter than honey? And what is stronger than a lion? and he said unto them, If ye had not plowed with my heifer, ye had not found out my riddle. And the Spirit of the Lord came upon him, and he went down to Ashkelon, and slew thirty men of them, and took their spoil, and gave change of garments unto them which expounded the riddle. And his anger was kindled, and he went up to his father's house. Judges 14:17- 19

As you can see, Samson lost the bet. He didn't even have 30 sheets and 30 pair of clothes to pay his debt. He had to go down to

Ashkelon and slay 30 men to get what he owed. This is what he had to do in order to keep his word.

The message behind this story tells us what gambling leads to. Whether it's in incarceration or on the streets, gambling can lead to violence. Many fights can often occur over gambling.

People have lost thousands of dollars that do not belong to them in casinos and have done some pretty wild things to get it back. This story serves as a warning to those who gamble. Especially with money they do not have.

God wants us to live a pure and holy life and He wants us to enjoy the things that He has given us. It is hard to enjoy anything when we allow sin into our lives because it drives us to anger, and jealousy, and hatred; these are works of the flesh. Those who gamble sow to the flesh and will also reap the consequences thereof.

Gambling is one of those things that will drive a person to anger. In verse 19 it says that Samson's "anger was kindled." Samson was angry because of his wife's betrayal and because of his loss.

Samson's debt also put him in a position to break his Nazarite vow. Samson was not supposed to touch the dead, yet he slayed the men in Ashkelon and took the clothes off their dead bodies to get thirty sets of garments for those who expounded the riddle.

The Lord has also revealed to us a double meaning behind this scripture. You see, a riddle usually has a double meaning and the Word of God is double edged as well. In this scripture, Samson was playing the role of a bully. He was prowling upon these Philistines to devour but ended up getting devoured himself. Out of the eater comes meat and out of the strong something sweet. Although Samson was speaking of the lion and the honey. he was now being an un witted pawn of the enemy as he sought to devour. He was the eater but with this unfortunate change of events he became meat for the Philistines. Samson was a strong guy and out of him came their winnings.

In this section of the text we find Samson taking a pretty big loss. It is true that Samson was predestined to make war with the

Philistines. God used Samson's anger to motivate him to do what he was created for: "And we know that all things work together for good to them that love God, to them who are the called according to *his* purpose" (Romans 8:28).

It is the same for all those who have ever had a problem with gambling. All who have felt the frustration from losing. God will use that anger to motivate you to hate the sin of gambling and to come against it. The Spirit of God will come over you to destroy the spirit of gambling which is indeed a spirit of addiction.

Samson was created to deliver his people from the hands of the Philistines. Perhaps you are also predestined to do the same. The Philistines represent the evil spirits that are influential to gambling and many other evil behaviors.

If you can rise above the spirit of addiction then you will become an inspiration to those who are still in bondage. Once you conquer the spirit of gambling, others who have seen you many years in casinos or at the spade table will be motivated by your God given strength to overcome and you can lead them to do it as well.

Samson was raised up to be a judge yet he struggled with the same sins as everyone else. It is important that we do not grow judgmental of those who are still stuck in the same sins we have overcome. Instead we should understand their struggles and fight for them.

Judge not and you shall not be judged. These judges were raised up to bring justice to God's people, not to place judgement. If we want to bring justice, we have to start with the man in the mirror.

But Samson's wife was given to his companion, whom he had used as his friend. Judges 14:20

But it came to pass within a while after, in the time of wheat harvest, that Samson visited his wife with a kid; and he said, I will go in to my wife into the chamber. But her father would not suffer him to go in. Judges 15: 1

After Samson got over the whole betrayal incident he was finally ready to enjoy his wife. The young goat he took was a present that he would offer so that he may be reconciled with her.

When he arrived to her house, Samson found himself at a closed door. Her father did not let him in.

One thing we will learn in life about closed doors is that Jesus is always behind them. When there is an open door it is Jesus who is allowing us to go through. He opens doors that no man can shut and closes doors that no man can open.

There are some doors that God will allow us to walk through for a season but when He gets ready to shift something in our lives these doors will begin to close. No matter how hard we try to get through it we will not be able to. The sooner we realize it, the sooner we will be able to adapt to the transition that we are going through.

Even though it was of God for Samson to marry the Philistine woman (Judges14:4) it was also God closing the door to the relationship. If God really wanted Samson to stay with her then the door would have stayed open.

It was not God's intentions for Samson to stay with this uncircumcised Philistine woman just to go on living a carnal life. Scripture says that the marriage was of God because He sought an occasion against the Philistines.

As we discussed previously, the marriage was an alternative plan to get Samson to start moving towards his purpose. His mission was to begin delivering Israel out of the hand of the Philistines. Therefore when the time was right God closed the door on Samson so that he would start moving towards the purpose for which he was called. This is the reason why Samson could not go in to his wife's chambers to lay with her.

And her father said, I verily thought that thou hadst utterly hated her; therefore I gave her to thy companion: is not her younger sister fairer than she? take her, I pray thee, instead of her. Judges 15:2

Her father had given Samson's wife to one of his companions from the wedding feast. He claimed to have thought Samson hated her after what happened at the wedding and was now offering up her little sister as a replacement.

When reading this story the best thing to do is to look at it from every angle and allow God to reveal as much truth to us as possible. We can see God's hand working in a mysterious way over Samson's life to bring about the purpose from which he was called. We can also see the Lord setting an example through Samson so that we may learn from it.

He sets an example by showing us what happens when a believer becomes unequally yoked with an unbeliever. It becomes a mess. Samson's wife ended up with his companion. If the woman was God fearing she would've never left the wedding with another man. Even though it was her father who gave her to another, she still had the choice herself to be loyal to her husband.

When a woman is God fearing her whole focus is on pleasing God, therefore perversion and fornication are far from her. A God fearing woman is virtuous and she holds the house down for her husband and her children, making their lives better while serving God.

On the other hand, the woman Samson married was not much of a housewife. The message behind his relationship teaches us the dangers of being unequally yoked.

Samson was stripped of his joy because the woman he loved was with another man. The woman left with his companion. On account of the situation, anger and jealousy began to surface and Samson started to act upon it.

And Samson said concerning them, Now shall I be more blameless than the Philistines, though I do them a displeasure. Judges 15:3

As you can see, God knew exactly what to do to stir up Samson so that the mission would be underway. Samson was angry and he intended to retaliate.

It is very important that we do not misinterpret the scriptures. Samson was chosen to do this very thing. He was chosen to fight against the Philistines just like we are chosen to fight against evil. God has called us to battle against sin. We should be recognizing sin as the enemy. When we think of every time that it has robbed us of our joy we should be disgusted. We ought to be angry with it. That is a righteous anger.

During the time of Samson's life the Philistines were portrayed to be Israel's most dangerous enemies. We have to look at the Philistines from a spiritual standpoint to understand that the Philistines represent evil spirits that are connected to, and also encourage the very same sin that has so easily ensnared the people of that time and also of our own. They move through the weaker elements of this world. They work through unbelievers of the opposite sex to entice God's children.

It has been said, by so many people, that Samson had an anger problem. This may be true but in this particular verse he was angry because his wife was given to someone else. Who wouldn't be angry in a situation like this?

The Bible says, "be angry and do not sin (Ephesians 4:26)." If you take your anger out on the people around you for what you are going through then you'd be wrong, but it is different to be angry with the evil that has stripped you of your joy. Especially when the same evil has been destroying so many people's lives around you. It is ok to be angry at the sin that causes you to stumble. Fight against it. It is okay to be angry with evil spirits that work through others causing discord and unbelief. It is okay to be angry with the drug addiction. It is ok to point your anger in the direction of wickedness and fight against it. Be angry but do not sin.

It is important to know who our enemy is and where we are supposed to direct our anger. We are at war with sin and evil spirits. That is exactly what the Philistines represent. We are not at war with the people who bring offense into our lives. We have to forgive them but we wage war with the evil spirits that influence them to bring offense.

And Samson went and caught three hundred foxes, and took firebrands, and turned tail to tail, and put a firebrand in the midst between two tails. And when he had set the brands on fire, he let them go into the standing corn of the Philistines, and burnt up both the shocks, and also the standing corn, with the vineyards and olives. Judges 15:4-5

Foxes were pretty common in the land of Canaan and it is not surprising that Samson was able to catch as many as he did. Perhaps he set traps while God brought forth the animals. It was God who caused the animals to come to the ark for Noah and it was also God that filled the disciples' nets with fish and it could have been the same in Samson's situation.

The Bible says that he caught three hundred foxes. Once again we find the number three hundred. A number that has a connection with the number three which is closely associated with the Holy Trinity. It took God three days to rise from the dead, so therefore we know that the number indicates divine deliverance. It was God's hand behind the gathering of these foxes. If God has a specific mission for anyone to accomplish, He will be there to help.

In Song of Solomon there is a scripture that speaks about foxes having the ability to spoil vines. In this scripture the poetry was used to bring guidelines to a relationship between a man and woman, as well as the relationship between the Lord and mankind: "Take us the foxes, the little foxes, that spoil the vines: for our vines have tender grapes" (Song of Solomon 2:15).

It has been said that the little foxes in Song of Solomon represent "little problems." These are things that can spoil the vine. The little things that come between our relationship with God. If there is any little thing in our lives that can be considered a problem in our relationship with God or our spouses we must remove them before they become big problems and spoil the vines.

Jesus is the true vine and there is nothing that can actually ruin Him, but it is our relationship with Him that these foxes can ruin. The connection between us and the vine is precious. There is something beautiful that begins to grow inside of us as we stay connected to Him. We build our relationship and we begin bearing much fruit. The grapes become tender and our relationship flourishes. At this point we will experience love, joy, and peace all at a level we never thought possible.

Although our relationship is beginning to flourish and blossom we must always be aware of the little foxes because they can spoil the vines. Foxes are known to be cunning and clever animals. The little foxes can be looked at metaphorically as clever strategies that the enemy uses to destroy what precious things are growing in our lives.

When Samson caught the foxes he was using a clever strategy

to bring problems to the enemy. These foxes would destroy their harvest.

According to Matthew 9:38 the harvest is the souls of the people that belong to Jesus. The truth is, Satan mimics everything that God does and he is doing his best to get a harvest of souls as well. It would be a good thing to put a stop to that. The best way to do it is with Holy Ghost fire.

The foxes were set on fire. The fire represents the Spirit of God. The best way for the man of God to destroy the enemy's harvest is by setting people's lives on fire with the Holy Spirit.

Is your soul on fire for Jesus? If so, then you can destroy the enemy's harvest. Since the moment that you have been set ablaze by the Holy Spirit you have posed a threat to the enemy's harvest. This fire that you have is very contagious. Everywhere you go that fire is burning and people can be touched by the flames.

If we apply everything that we learn from the scriptures and do all that God tells us to do then we can keep the fire going in our soul. Stay excited about worship and be willing to go the extra mile to make an impact.

No retreats, no regrets, no remorse. Take everything you can from the enemy. He was relentless when he came against you. He was merciless. Give no place to the devil. Leave no room for defeat.

Samson tied the foxes' tails together and he sent them out by two. It was a really good idea because it would keep them in the field longer. They wouldn't be able to run away because they were tied together nor would they be able to go into their holes. They would stay in the field longer running circles.

This was a good move on Samson's behalf. He went after their harvest. He burned up their food supply and crippled their economy.

Then the Philistines said, Who hath done this? And they answered, Samson, the son in law of the Timnite, because he had taken his wife, and given her to his companion. And the Philistines came up, and burnt her and her father with fire. Judges 15:6

The fire that Samson's wife was burned with was not Holy Ghost fire. Her fire represents the fire of hell. The very reason why she betrayed Samson in the first place was to avoid getting her and her father burned.

When the Philistines threatened to burn her and her father she persistently pressed Samson for answers with the intent to betray him. Yet her and her father still got burned.

This goes to show that when a person uses deceit to avoid affliction, they usually have to face it anyway. It was because of her deceit that she got thrown into the fire that she was trying to escape.

In the book of Daniel, three of God's soldiers were thrown into the furnace for not bowing to the image of Nebuchadnezzar. They did not fear the fiery furnace. They did not cower. Instead, they trusted in God and though they were thrown into the flames they were delivered from the heat thereof.

We should never cower nor use deceit to escape from something that might be painful. Instead, we must always trust our God to get us through.

Fire can also be looked at as a way of purification: "I will bring the third part through the fire, and will refine them as silver is refined, and will try them as gold is tried." (Zechariah 13:9). We go through pain, we suffer tribulation and we endure hardships, and through these things we grow. This is the process of purification. By trusting God we grow, but when we try to avoid it we face it regardless.

And Samson said unto them, Though ye have done this, yet will I be avenged of you, and after that I will cease. And he smote them hip and thigh with a great slaughter: and he went down and dwelt in the top of the rock Etam. Judges 15:7-8

Samson said that he would not stop fighting with the Philistines until he got his vengeance. He was angry on account of his wife. He was using his anger to come against the Philistines.

God had already foreseen this. He knew He could carry out His own will even through Samson's anger and selfish ambition. Once again that is why Samson's marriage was of God.

When a person is chosen by God to carry out a specific task he will then be ushered into his calling at the appointed time and season. The Lord knows exactly how to get that person to do His will. Whether they know it or not, God's will shall be done.

This time Samson went in amongst the Philistines physically and smote them hip and thigh. Hip and thigh was an expression that was commonly used among the Jews. A thigh has a lot of meat on it and the hip has hardly any. Therefore the phrase means big and small, high and low, or good and bad. Samson went in amongst the Philistines on a rampage and slaughtered hip and thigh. Everyone in sight.

Samson started the battle that he was destined to fight but as soon as he felt satisfied with vengeance he stopped and retreated to the cave of Etam. The moment he decided to start this fight he should have been prepared to battle until the very end. In the same way, when anyone decides to take a stand and fight the good fight they must be prepared to do it until the very end.

After his attack on the Philistines, Samson retreated to hide in a cave. It is usually in places like this where the men of God are able to seek out God and hear from Him. It is possible that while Samson was alone in this cave that he went to God with his pain and his frustration over the situation with his wife.

He would've had complaints because he couldn't really understand why he was going through all this pain over his wife and he definitely had some requests.

He needed God's help to get by. This cave may have served as a prayer closet that would prepare him for what was going to happen next. When the battles of life get so heavy on us it is important for us to retreat to the prayer closet as well. Find a cave or quiet place where we can talk to God and hear that still calm voice and receive revelations.

Then the Philistines went up, and pitched in Judah, and spread themselves in Lehi. Judges 15:9

While Samson was in the rock of Etam, the Philistines went and camped in Juda to bind him. They had soldiers spread throughout Lehi, which was in the territory of Juda.

Keep in mind that the Philistines ruled over Israel at the time. That is the reason why God was raising up Samson to deliver the people.

Samson had already started the mission but the moment he stopped fighting, things got worse. His own people had to deal with the Philistines on account of his actions. They were in the land of Juda looking for him.

And the men of Judah said, Why are ye come up against us? And they answered, To bind Samson are we come up, to do to him as he hath done to us. Then three thousand men of Judah went to the top of the rock Etam, and said to Samson, Knowest thou not that the Philistines are rulers over us? what is this that thou hast done unto us? And he said unto them, As they did unto me, so have I done unto them. Judges 15:10-11

The Philistines came to bind Samson and the men of Judah decided to help them. They were afraid because the Philistines ruled over them at the time and therefore they did not want any problems.

They were fearful. Samson was in effect their token of peace so they decided to hand him over. Apparently they knew exactly where he was hiding.

And they said unto him, We are come down to bind thee, that we may deliver thee into the hand of the Philistines. And Samson said unto them, Swear unto me, that ye will not fall upon me yourselves. And they spake unto him, saying, No; but we will bind thee fast, and deliver thee into their hand: but surely we will not kill thee. And they bound him with two new cords, and brought him up from the rock. Judges: 15:12-13

Instead of letting his people suffer hostility or ill treatment at the hands of the enemy, Samson decided to hand himself over. Some people would have ran and hid but Samson was willing to lay his life down for his friends. There is no greater love than this. His actions in this portion of scripture portrayed a Christ like character. Jesus laid His life down when His own people bound Him and crucified Him.

As Samson went out bound before his enemies we can picture him as a sheep getting led to the slaughter. Handed over by his own people, we can picture Samson walking bound and defeated as he gets turned over into the hands of his enemies.

And when he came unto Lehi, the Philistines shouted against him: and the Spirit of the Lord came mightily upon him, and the cords that were upon his arms became as flax that was burnt with fire, and his bands loosed from off his hands. Judges 15:14

He may have looked like a defeated man to the Philistines and even in the eyes of Judah. But the Spirit of the Lord came upon Samson mightily so that the ropes around his arms burned as flax. The cords on his arms became like thread that is hit with a lighter.

That which had bound Samson was now done away with. Where the Spirit of the Lord is, there is freedom. The man that looked defeated was about to rise up in victory.

The Spirit of the Lord came mightily upon Samson. God was still with him and God still wanted to use him.

And he found a new jawbone of an ass, and put forth his hand, and took it, and slew a thousand men therewith. And Samson said, With the jawbone of an ass, heaps upon heaps, with the jaw of an ass have I slain a thousand men. Judges 15:15-16

When the bands were loosened from Samson's hands, he reached for the only thing in sight. All that was available to him was the jawbone of a donkey.

Samson was willing to fight back. He may have been In a state of emptiness and brokenness when he was walking bound before his enemies but when he realized his pitiful state he refused to stay in it. He felt the urge to fight back and he did.

It was God who provided the jawbone and the strength for Samson to break free. God will always provide a way out of temptation that is common to man.

If we ever find ourselves in a situation like the one Samson was in, we will have to refuse to stay in it. We will have to be willing to fight back in order to get out of bondage and rise above our circumstances.

If we would be willing to fight back, then God will do great things on our behalf. It doesn't matter what we have been bound to, we can always overcome.

With the jawbone of the donkey, Samson piled heaps upon heaps of dead bodies on top of dead bodies. In the New International Version, it interprets verse 16 like this; "With a donkey's jawbone I have made donkeys of them. With a donkey's jawbone I have killed a thousand men."

In the Bible the word donkey is used metaphorically. A donkey is a really stubborn and foolish animal. Sometimes people are compared to donkeys when they act stubborn and foolishly. Samson made donkeys out of his enemies (he made fools of them).

Donkeys are stubborn animals. It is hard to get them to move when they are fearful or when they prefer to stay put. It is true that many people act the same way.

Samson was a particularly stubborn individual. He was so stuck on this Philistine woman that he was hardly moving forward in his calling. We could see that his focus was more on the uncircumcised Philistine woman than on his God given purpose. Many times in scripture we will find Samson acting a lot like a donkey. Yet despite all his stubbornness, God still chose to use him: "But God hath chosen the foolish things of the world to confound the wise; and God hath chosen the weak things of the world to confound the things which are mighty" (1 Corinthians 1:27).

Samson had a lot in common with the people of Israel. They were also a stiff-necked and stubborn people. Perhaps it could have been a reflection of his leadership. The type of leadership we portray reflects through the people around us.

If we sit in frustration over the stubbornness of others, then maybe we have to set a better example. If we thrive to be better leaders, then we will get better results.

Many of us can relate to Samson because we have struggled with the same sins as he did. There are people who have a relationship with God and still have a tendency to get unequally yoked with nonbelievers. God wants us to move further into our calling but when we are in a state of stubbornness we cannot move forward. Stubborn people just lay there like donkeys.

The jawbone of a donkey is metaphorical to the mouthpiece of a stubborn man. In the midst of prayer and in the midst of declaring God's word even the most stubborn people can find victory.

We must refuse to stay in a defeated state. We fight our battles by trusting in God's word and speaking it over our lives. God's word is our weapon of offense. We recite it, we proclaim it, and we use it while we pray with all our hearts.

The jawbone of a donkey is all that was available to Samson. He was willing to use whatever he could to slay his enemies. Without hesitation he grabbed ahold of this jawbone and fought valiantly.

Donkeys are also metaphorical to how far God is willing to go in order to carry out his own plans. The book of judges is not the first time in scripture that God uses the jawbone of a donkey to accomplish His will.

In the book of Numbers there is a story about a prophet named Balaam who was on a mission, riding a donkey to curse the Israelites. When the donkey sees an angel of God in his path he lay down so that Balaam could not proceed. Balaam started beating this stubborn animal but it just lay there. At this point the Lord opens the donkey's mouth to rebuke Balaam for his iniquity. God uses the jawbone of a donkey to rebuke the prophet with a man's voice, and keep him from proceeding with his own madness (Numbers 22:21-30).

In New Testament times we find Jesus making His triumphant entry on the back of a donkey (Matthew 25:1-11). He sent his disciples to set loose the donkey because He had need of it. In the same manner God loosened the hands of Samson so that he could triumph over his enemies. God will also loosen His people from bondage when He decides to make a triumphant entry into their lives: "Tell ye the daughter of Sion, Behold, thy King cometh unto thee, meek, and sitting upon an ass, and a colt the foal of an ass" (Matthew 21:5).

God made a triumphant entry when he loosened Samson's hands to slay his enemies. It was God who empowered Samson to get this victory and it was God who got the glory.

When God first comes to us we are stiff-necked and stubborn people but He shows up triumphantly. Metaphorically speaking, He makes a triumphant entrance riding an on the back of an donkey. He chooses the foolish things of this world to confound the wise and He gets Glory by doing so.

Keep in mind that God wants us to move forward, to grow, to

progress, to mature. He doesn't want us to stay acting stubborn. He wants us be better people and accomplish bigger things. If we continue in our stubbornness all we are going to do is put ourselves in a position like Samson who was bound by his own people and oppressed by his enemies.

In Zechariah 9:9 there is a prophecy about Jesus making His triumphant entry riding on a donkey. Jesus fulfilled this prophecy when he came to us the first time. In Revelation 19:11-16 there is a prophecy about the second coming of Christ. Next time He will be returning on a white horse.

White symbolizes purity; it is the same color that all of His saints will be clothed in. It represents cleanliness from sin.

Though many of us are a little rough around the edges now, God can bring us to the point where we are well disciplined, well mannered, and squared away just like any military soldier. We have to get past the stubborn phase in our walk with the Lord and graduate from it.

When Jesus comes to us in our beginning stages we are like the donkey from which He made His triumphant entry, but as we wait for the second coming of Christ we will be a lot less comparable to the donkey and a lot more comparable to the white horse. The difference in the character of a horse and a donkey is that the horse is a lot more obedient and a lot less stubborn. A horse will charge into battle at the prompting of its master. Horses are a lot bigger and stronger than donkeys.

And it came to pass, when he had made an end of speaking, that he cast away the jawbone out of his hand, and called that place Ramathlehi. And he was sore athirst, and called on the Lord, and said, Thou hast given this great deliverance into the hand of thy servant: and now shall I die for thirst, and fall into the hand of the uncircumcised? But God clave an hollow place that was in the jaw, and there came water thereout; and when he had drunk, his spirit came again, and he revived: wherefore he called the name thereof Enhakkore, which is in Lehi unto this day. Judges 15:17-19.

Samson called the place Ramathlehi, which is jawbone hill. He named the place after his victory with the jawbone. Yet it was not the jawbone that brought this great victory to Samson.

When the battle was finally over Samson gave reverence to God. He recognized that deliverance came from God alone. It was God who delivered the Philistines into the hand of His servant. It is God alone who continues to deliver those whom He loves out of the hands of the enemy.

Samson was in there swinging the jawbone of a donkey but it was God who strengthened him. The Spirit of the Lord came mightily upon Samson. Samson didn't stand a chance on his own. It was all because of God that Samson was victorious.

The Bible does not say that Samson was trained in martial arts or that was he a heavyweight golden glove boxer. It doesn't say that he was a bodybuilder or that he was physically fit. For all we know Samson could have been built like the average man.

Every time that Samson was able to pull off something amazing it was because the Spirit of the lord was on him. The strength of Samson was a spiritual strength.

Jesus said in Acts 1:8 that you would receive power when the Holy Spirit comes upon you. He is telling you the same thing today. The Spirit that God gives you will empower you to perform signs and miracles. It will empower you to accomplish your God given purpose. It will empower you to trample on demonic forces and it will also empower you to live victorious.

God will supply the strength that we need to accomplish great things. All we have to do is put an effort behind it. The battles we go through as Christian soldiers are not easy. Samson fought for his life but the Lord strengthened him to do it. He fought hard, to the point of dehydration. He was thirsty. He needed water. Water represents life. Where there is water there is life.

Perhaps Samson was an empty vessel and he just needed to be filled. Jesus said blessed are those who hunger and thirst for righteousness. It could be that Samson was thirsty for righteousness. He had begun to drift away from God on account of the uncircumcised Philistine but now he was coming back to his first love. He was thirsty for righteousness. He yearned to get back into right standing with the King of kings. He was thirsty for living waters.

After drinking the water that God provided for him he was refreshed, and he revived. He had come back to life. In this particular verse we see the soul of Samson being restored.

And he judged Israel in the days of the Philistines twenty years. Judges 15:20

God revived Samson and gave him a purpose. Samson was now leading God's people. He was finally walking in the calling that God had for him. Samson led the people of Israel in the days of the Philistines for twenty years. God wants you to lead the people today. Whether it is the spirit of the Philistines or any other spirit oppressing the people.

Then went Samson to Gaza, and saw there an harlot, and went in unto her. Judges16:1

We can learn a lot from the character of Samson. One of the main things we can learn from him is what not to do.

After judging and leading Israel for twenty years Samson fell back into his sinful nature. He should have been moving forward in his walk with the Lord. Graduating from a leader to a conqueror. From a Moses to a Joshua but instead he backslid.

Samson fell short of God's glory. We all fall short of God's glory. We all make mistakes but when we do, we are supposed to learn from them. A man who makes no mistakes knows nothing. Mistakes are part of the learning process for every child of God but from the looks of it Samson never really learned from his.

His first mistake was when he went into enemy territory and found his wife. Now he is back in enemy territory messing around with another uncircumcised Philistine.

Scripture says, "Samson went to Gaza (Judges 16:1)." Gaza was one of the chief Philistine cities. He wasn't just passing by the city nor did he accidentally end up there. He went to Gaza on purpose. While he was there he saw a harlot and he slept with her.

When Samson went down to Timnath he found a wife and now that he went down to Gaza he found a harlot. The fact of the matter is that both times he went into enemy territory he was distracted by these uncircumcised Philistine women.

God said that He would be with you wherever you go but that doesn't mean that you can just go anywhere. He promised to give you every place that you set the sole of your foot but that is because He is the one ordering your steps. God will not order your steps into a triple X movie theater. He will not direct your path into the trap house nor any other place where people are posted up getting high all day.

It would be unwise to think that you can go to these kind of places and hang out without falling into sin, especially if you have struggled in these areas before. That would be stepping outside of God's will. You know the saying: "if you stay at the barbershop long enough you will get a haircut."

Samson walked away from the light to fornicate with a harlot and found himself in a dark place. Most definitely God was screaming out to Samson, saying, "No, son, you're going the wrong way!" but Samson was acting stubborn again. He was deep in enemy territory. This goes to show how far his lustful desires took him. Far enough to defile his temple.

A harlot could be considered the same thing as a prostitute, which is bought at a price to have sexual relations. Prostitution is most likely far more common these days than in the days of Samson.

Truth is, many of us have been down to Gaza in past times. We have struggled with the same sin that Samson did. The pleasure of sex. Sleeping with members of the opposite sex who we are not married to is a sinful act and so many of us have failed in this area.

In Christ we find satisfaction that far outweighs the pleasure of sex and any other pleasure known to man. We find purpose and fulfillment in Christ. He gives us new desires and removes the old ones.

As we begin to grow in Christ it should be that we never want to go down to Gaza again. He strengthens us so that we can trample on the spirit of the Philistines. We can trample on adultery, fornication, and lust. These are the sins that Samson struggled with when he came into contact with the Philistines. That is how we know what the Philistines represent.

They lorded over Israel at the time and in reality they still lord over many people to this day. It could be that God is raising you up to fight against them and bring deliverance through Jesus Christ. Let Him use you.

There are so many people in bondage because they have given themselves over to the lust of the flesh. Fornication, gambling, and drug addictions have gotten the best of a lot of good soldiers. These things were all present in Samson's time.

Drugs fall into the same category as alcohol. Some people say that Samson broke his vow by drinking liquor at his wedding. Although there is no solid evidence of that in scripture it could've been a possibility because the temptation was always there.

Sex, drugs, and gambling run hand in hand. It is a lifestyle that so many people are all too familiar with. It can be a struggle to break free from these things but Jesus is the answer.

The root cause of Samson's mistake wasn't recorded. But if we dig a little deeper perhaps we could figure out the reason why Samson fell into temptation.

The Bible says, "Watch and pray, that ye enter not into temptation: the spirit indeed *is* willing, but the flesh *is* weak (Matthew 26:41)." Without prayer our relationship with God begins to weaken, and because of this, it is possible for sin to overthrow the man of God. According to Matthew 26:41 if we stay in constant prayer it will be a lot less likely for us to fall.

Perhaps Samson had not been in constant prayer when he fell. Maybe he allowed something else to take the place of his prayer life. As Christians we should never let anything take the place of our prayer life unless we want to fall into the danger of temptation.

We have to be careful nowadays with all the things that could be a distraction to our prayer life. With all this technology, phones, movies and video games we have to learn to properly balance our lives because these things can also distract us from prayer and from walking righteously. If we start allowing other things to take up the time we should be spending with our king, then we place ourselves in danger of falling into temptation.

It is possible that Samson got tired of waiting on God to give him a suitable helper. He burned with passion and it drove him to fill his lustful desires. Samson had a problem when it came to women. He did not know how to choose them.

Another thing to consider is that Samson was always by himself. Scripture never talks about him being around other believers or soldiers. Fellowship is important. Without the gathering of the people we are a lot more likely to fall into sin: "A person standing alone can be attacked and defeated, but two can stand back-to-back and conquer. Three are even better, for a triple-braided cord is not easily broken" (Ecclesiastes 4:12 NLT).

We were created to walk in unity. To carry each other's burdens and keep one another from falling. If we seclude ourselves from the body of Christ then we have no backup. All the other judges led an army out to war but Samson did things alone. Perhaps this is part of the reason he fell short so many times.

There are so many people out there that need guidance. Your fire is contagious and people will be drawn to you but the moment you decide to go back into the sinful nature you are liable to cause damage to those who follow you. Samson's actions in this verse are the type that would cause damage to those who looked up to him spiritually. There is always someone watching who needs the right kind of leadership.

If you truly want to be a leader worth following then you have to live a holy and blameless life with perseverance. Don't give up. Don't turn back. Don't let the fire in your soul burn out. Take leadership seriously. Consider the souls of those who will come to know Christ because of your obedience. Do not cause your brother to stumble.

And it was told the Gazites, saying, Samson is come hither. And they compassed him in, and laid wait for him all night in the gate of the city, and were quiet all the night, saying, In the morning, when it is day, we shall kill him. And Samson lay till midnight, and arose at midnight, and took the doors of the gate of the city, and the two posts, and went away with them, bar and all, and put them upon his shoulders, and carried them up to the top of an hill that is before Hebron. Judges 16:2-3

Gaza was a fortified city with high walls and a large gate that was strong enough to withstand an attacking army. Many gates in ancient times were enormous. They were made of stone, iron, brass, or wood and they were usually covered with metal or at least reinforced with metal bands. The weight of these gates could have been anywhere from four to eight tons and could have taken up to twenty people to open and close them.

In those times, the city gates would stay open during the day so that the people who reside there could come and go as they pleased. At night the gates would close, just in case an enemy decided to attack. When the gates were closed there was no longer any way to enter or exit the city. You were in or you were out.

The gates in this scripture were literal but this incident was recorded to enlighten our spiritual understanding. There are many spiritual gates that people can pass through. Some are good and some are evil. Heaven has gates and Hell has gates as well.

There are also gates and doors that lead to the inner man. These entrances were designed so that the Holy Spirit can flow through us, and take up residency in us. When these doors and gates are left open to the wrong things evil and darkness will take it as an opportunity to move in. The strength of any fortress or city lies within the gates.

The gates that Samson entered to fornicate with this prostitute were spiritual as much as they were literal. These gates represent the wide gates that lead to destruction. This conclusion comes from the fact that he entered them to fornicate: Enter ye in at the strait gate:

"for wide *is* the gate, and broad *is* the way, that leadeth to destruction, and many there be which go in thereat:" (Matthew 7:13).

Samson entered into the wide gates when he was drawn away by his own lustful desires and enticed. He was headed for destruction in his search for pleasure. He fed his fleshly desire only to find a fleeting sense of gratification.

While he was busy fornicating the gates closed in on him and he was trapped behind enemy lines. To make matters worse his enemies knew he was there. They found out that he had come to their territory and they laid in wait for him. They compassed him round about with murderous plots.

These results are to be expected for anyone who decides to touch the things that God forbids. They shall be exposed and marked for ruin.

It was at the darkest hours of the night (midnight) when Samson rose up to carry out one the greatest miracles of his life.

First he managed to get past the soldiers that surrounded him. Then he took the doors of the gate of the city, and the two posts, and went away with them, bar and all, and put them upon his shoulders, and carried them up to the top of a hill that is before Hebron.

Hebron was around 36 miles away and around 3,200 feet higher in altitude. Not only did Samson make an escape, he also possessed the gates of his enemies.

In Genesis 22:17 God made a promise to Abraham that his seed would be multiplied and that it would possess the gates of his enemies. Samson was of that seed both literally and spiritually. Samson was of the bloodline of Abraham and he was also a man of faith. He had a relationship with God and he knew that God could get him out of this mess.

It was God who gave Samson the ability to get past the soldiers who surrounded him. It was God who gave him the strength to carry the gates that weighed far more than he could even lift. By the grace of God, Samson was able to perform this miracle. Despite his errors, God had mercy, and gave him the strength to do the impossible.

This scripture reveals to us the mercies and the grace of God. It shows His love towards us. Even when we turn our backs on Him, He is still willing to reach out and rescue us from destruction.

It doesn't mean that we should go put ourselves in a predicament just to see God's power. It means that if we are in any kind of predicament, we still have hope.

Samson rose up at midnight. He didn't stay down. He got back up. He was at a point of repentance and that is why he was able to possess the gates of his enemies. It was because God intervened.

Give thanks to the LORD; for he is good: for his mercy endureth forever. Give praise to our God because He makes a way when there is no way. The gates of hell will not prevail.

31

And it came to pass afterward, that he loved a woman in the valley of Sorek, whose name was Delilah. Judges 16:4

Have you ever been in love with someone who does not love you? Someone who plays you, uses you, and constantly mistreats you? Someone who tries to break you down mentally and emotionally?

This is the kind of relationship Samson got himself into. He didn't know how to pick his women.

He loved this woman whose name was Delilah but there is no mention of her loving him. He was investing in a relationship that had no return.

There are many who have been in similar relationships. Toxic ones. The type that seem to be good in the beginning but in the end they turn out to be so deadly.

There is no discussion about a marriage nor does the scripture tell us that he was properly courting this woman. Therefore we know that Samson was involved in a sinful relationship.

This relationship took place after the fact that he had already fallen into the sin of fornication with the harlot in Gaza. There was a connection between the two. This goes to show that when a person allows sin to come into their life it gradually increases.

It could've been because he was not immediately punished for his sin in Gaza that he continued to compromise. Sin was now taking root in his heart and beginning to grow.

Throughout the story of Samson we find him falling short time and time again, yet there was no immediate consequence for his actions. His behavior was repeated without penalty. Therefore Samson went through a gradual process where his unacceptable practices and standards became acceptable and normal to him. He began to believe that God would still be with him even though he was living a life of constant and deliberate sin.

At this point, if we decide to trade the truth in for a lie, God will hand us over to the sinful desires of our hearts. Not only does sexual impurity defile the temple of the living God it also leads to spiritual blindness and even death.

And the lords of the Philistines came up unto her, and said unto her, Entice him, and see wherein his great strength lieth, and by what means we may prevail against him, that we may bind him to afflict him; and we will give thee every one of us eleven hundred pieces of silver. Judges 16:5

The lords who came up to Delilah were more than likely the leaders of the Philistine cities which were identified as Gaza, Ashdod, Ashkelon, Ekron and Gath. Five cities in total. Five leaders in total. These were men of power and rank. They made an irresistible bribe of 1,100 pieces of silver each, which is a total of 5,500 pieces of silver altogether.

They offered Delilah money to seduce him into to revealing the secrets of his great strength. They wanted to know the means by which they could prevail against him. They wanted to know what made him so strong so that they could find a way to weaken him.

They wanted to overpower him so that they could bind him and afflict him.

The things that took place for Samson in the natural were written to give us an idea of what goes on in the spiritual. We have enemies.

There are demonic forces that are trying to find a way to bind and afflict God's children. They will use other people just like the Philistines were using Delilah to figure out our weaknesses. They will use other people (just like the Philistines were using Delilah) to figure out our weaknesses. They will approach us, test us and even attack us in many different areas but only through observation can they recognize our weakness.

The devil doesn't automatically know our weaknesses. He comes to a conclusion of what they are as he studies our behavior. God is the only one who truly knows us inside and out. He knows our thoughts and the intentions of our heart, the devil doesn't.

It is through our actions and through the confession of our mouth that the enemy can get a glimpse of what's going on inside of us. Everything we do flows from the heart and out of the abundance thereof the mouth speaks.

If the devil plants seeds of bitterness in your life he will know if it takes root by your actions and your words. He will make evil suggestions and he will even broadcast certain attitudes into your mind to see how you respond. He will use others to attack you while he examines your reactions, but he only knows your weakness through observation.

In the same way the Philistines knew that Samson had a weakness with women because of observation. They had seen what measures he took over his wife in Timnath. They saw him risk his life over the harlot in Gaza. Therefore they knew Delilah was their ticket to get to him.

If the devil attacks you in a certain area and he sees you stumble on the account, he will then continue working through that same angle to bind you and afflict you. He is looking for a breech to get in to your life and destroy you. He has been studying you for a really long time. He is trying to find a way to weaken you to overthrow you and to subdue you.

And Delilah said to Samson, Tell me, I pray thee, wherein thy great strength lieth, and wherewith thou mightest be bound to afflict thee. And Samson said unto her, If they bind me with seven green withs that were never dried, then shall I be weak, and be as another man. Then the lords of the Philistines brought up to her seven green withs which had not been dried, and she bound him with them. Now there were men lying in wait, abiding with her in the chamber. And she said unto him, The Philistines be upon thee, Samson. And he brake the withs, as a thread of tow is broken when it toucheth the fire. So his strength was not known. And Delilah said unto Samson, Behold, thou hast mocked me, and told me lies: now tell me, I pray thee, wherewith thou mightest be bound. And he said unto her, If they bind me fast with new ropes that never were occupied, then shall I be weak, and be as another man. Delilah therefore took new ropes, and bound him therewith, and said unto him, The Philistines be upon thee, Samson. And there were liers in wait abiding in the chamber. And he brake them from off his arms like a thread. And Delilah said unto Samson, Hitherto thou hast mocked me, and told me lies: tell me wherewith thou mightest be bound. And he said unto her, If thou weavest the seven locks of my head with the web. And she fastened it with the pin, and said unto him, The Philistines be upon thee, Samson. And he awaked out of his sleep, and went away with the pin of the beam, and with the web. Judges 16:6-14

Samson must have recognized her true motives to some extent because he lied to her three times about the true source of his strength. It was out of wise judgment that he decided not to reveal his secrets at this point.

Delilah tried the green withs, the new ropes and she even wove seven locks in his head while he slept. She did it exactly how he told her to. Each time he would break free at the words, "Samson, the Philistines are upon you."

Scripture says that while she bound him there were men lying in wait, abiding with her in the chamber. They probably even supplied her with what she needed to bind him. She was basically setting him up.

This type of behavior happens everywhere in the world today. People pretend to be lovers and friends but when the opportune time comes they sell out, and set up even the closest people to them. People have been set up by their so-called lovers to get beaten, robbed, and even killed. It is a reality for many who choose to surround themselves with bad company while living sinful lives.

Sometimes the betrayal is done for money. Sometimes the betrayer does it to gain acceptance or trust from someone they really like. Either way, betrayal is always persuaded by devilish spirits.

In this passage the betrayal proceeds as the man of God falls into the trap of the immoral woman. We are always supposed to look at this spiritually to heed the true warning. The enemies that persuade the immoral woman are spiritual. The devil has been known to use the natural woman to set up the spiritual man.

Think of it as a woman who has bad spirits hidden within herself. They bring forth hidden motives with the intentions to bind and afflict the man of God.

When we speak about Delilah we do it from a spiritual standpoint. The spirit of Delilah moves through natural women who are willing to take the bribes from evil spirits to bind and afflict the man of God.

The devil will make promises and offers just like the Philistines did. When a woman takes up the offers she invites all these spirits to abide within herself.

The spirit of Delilah does not work alone. There are evil spirits lying in wait, abiding within her chambers. That is why the Bible tells us to keep our path far from the immoral woman and not to go near the door of her house (Proverbs 5:8). It is because within her chambers there is an ambush waiting happen.

The question is, what causes us to ignore the signs of a toxic woman? Could it be that we are so desperate to be loved that we do not pay attention to the inner character? Perhaps it was the fornication that Samson was really in love with and not the woman. What else could drive a man back in to the arms of someone who is constantly wounding him? Was it because she provided him a place to lay his head? A place that he went to get away from all the troubles in life, only to find more? These are questions that we have to ask ourselves so that we do not find ourselves in the same mess that Samson was in.

This story was not only written as a warning for the man of God but for the woman of God as well. The spirit of Delilah rests upon the immoral man as well. There are many ungodly men who the devil will use as he tries to bring down the woman who loves and serves the Lord also.

And she said unto him, How canst thou say, I love thee, when thine heart is not with me? thou hast mocked me these three times, and hast not told me wherein thy great strength lieth. And it came to pass, when she pressed him daily with her words, and urged him, so that his soul was vexed unto death; That he told her all his heart, and said unto her, There hath not come a razor upon mine head; for I have been a Nazarite unto God from my mother's womb: if I be shaven, then my strength will go from me, and I shall become weak, and be like any other man. And when Delilah saw that he had told her all his heart, she sent and called for the lords of the Philistines, saying, Come up this once, for he hath shewed me all his heart. Then the lords of the Philistines came up unto her, and brought money in their hand. Judges 16:15-18

Delilah used her words to press Samson daily. This means that she was nagging at him constantly with the objective to break him down mentally and emotionally. She was pushing him to prove his love for her only to destroy him in the process.

After many days of this treatment Samson became frustrated and sick unto death. She finally got to him and he told her all that was in his heart. This is a mistake that many of us have learned the hard way.

Not everyone who says they are on your side is really for you. There are some who say they love you but their hearts are far from you. The closer they get to you and the more they know about you the better their position to bring you harm. Telling them all that is in your heart gives them an opportunity to hurt you. It gives them an advantage over you.

Even fake friends will steal your ideas, step on your toes, and get you counted out of your own business deals. Never let the right hand know what the left is doing. Never tell your right hand man all that is in your heart unless prompted by the Lord.

Make sure you use the gift of discernment to test every spirit. Test the fruit of every so-called lover and friend. Make sure that they are filled with the right spirit before you reveal any of your secrets or plans. The biggest mistake Samson made was telling Delilah all his heart.

And she made him sleep upon her knees; and she called for a man, and she caused him to shave off the seven locks of his head; and she began to afflict him, and his strength went from him. Judges 16:19

Delilah put Samson to sleep before she made her move because in his sleep he was most vulnerable for the attack. In the same way the immoral woman will put the spiritual man to sleep so that he will be vulnerable for an attack by his spiritual enemies. For a spiritual man to fall asleep means that he has gone into a state of idleness.

It is at the point when we becomes prayer less that we begin to be spiritually unconscious. Only then does the enemy stand a chance to prevail with his attack.

That is why the immoral woman will try to put our focus on the flesh. If we begin to focus on carnal things our prayer life will start to dry out and without prayer we begin to drift away and doze off. This opens you up for a major attack by the enemy. That is why Jesus said "Why sleep ye? rise and pray, lest ye enter into temptation (Luke 22:46)."

When the seven locks of Samson's head were shaved off his strength went from him. It was gone. He became weak as any other man.

Although his hair really wasn't the source of his great strength it represented his commitment to God through the Nazarite vow. His hair was a symbol of his consecration to God. Although many would say that Samson had already began breaking his Nazarite vow long before the locks of his head were shaved, it was at this particular point that the Lord removed Himself from Samson's life.

The Lord is patient and merciful and full of love towards those that love Him. He gives chance after chance but when a person deliberately continues to compromise their commitment to Him, He will depart and leave that person to the things which he sets his heart after.

This portion of scripture also reminds us to keep the vows we make with God. It is better not to make a vow with the Lord than to make one and not follow through with it. If you have made a vow with the Lord it will be required of you.

The true source of Samson's strength came directly from his relationship with God. It did not come from his long hair. It is obvious that every believer finds their strength in Christ. It is a given for all who have intimacy with God to receive supernatural strength from him. We will not receive it by growing long hair. Hair is only used symbolically for strength.

White hair represents wisdom. The Bible also tells us that white hair is a crown of glory. As a person reaches a certain age they begin to get white hairs. With age comes wisdom and therefore a head full of white hair is also referred to as a crown of wisdom.

Let's consider the revelation of Jesus that was given to John on the a Island of Patmos. Scripture tells us that He had hairs as white as wool and as white as snow. This means He was girded with strength and wisdom. This does not have anything to do with race or ethnicity. The thickness and color of His hair represents His strength, His purity, and

His wisdom. The younger man glories in his strength and the older in his wisdom yet Christ has the glory of both.

When Jesus said "not a hair of your head will perish" He was speaking of our God given strength and wisdom. None of it will be taken. Even when it seems like the battles of life seem too tough to endure, not a hair on your head will perish. He knows the number of hairs on your head. He knows how much strength you have and how much wisdom you have obtained. He knows how much pain you can handle and how far you can go.

And she said, The Philistines be upon thee, Samson. And he awoke out of his sleep, and said, I will go out as at other times before, and shake myself. And he wist not that the Lord was departed from him. But the Philistines took him, and put out his eyes, and brought him down to Gaza, and bound him with fetters of brass; and he did grind in the prison house. Judges 16:20-21

Samson was spiritually blinded by his sin long before he ever lost his eyes physically. This is exactly what sin does to a person. It binds and it blinds. Without a vision people perish.

Samson had no vision within his compromise. He was walking blindly. He was no longer taking steps of faith, he was moving aimlessly in the wrong direction.

He thought that he would go out as before. He thought that he would be able to shake the Philistines off of him just as he had done in previous times. What he didn't realize was that the Spirit of God was no longer with him. He was attempting to do the work that he was called for without the God who called him. Imagine putting your hands to do the work of God without God. It just doesn't work out.

Samson was overthrown. The Philistines cut out his eyes, they bound him, and then they put him to grind in the prison house. Not only did they blind and bind him, they also enslaved him. He was grinding in the prison house. It is only because of his sin that that the enemy was able to put him in this position.

As we look at Samson's pitiful state we can get a clear understanding of what the devil wants to do to us. He wants to bind us, blind us, and enslave us. He aims to steal, kill, and destroy but he could only do so if we continue to compromise our faith.

32

Howbeit the hair of his head began to grow again after he was shaven. Judges 16:22

Eventually the hair on Samson's head began to grow. His strength was being renewed as he began to draw nigh unto God. Once again there was something beautiful taking place within his heart.

He was a man with a broken and contrite spirit. In his state of remorse he reflected back at what he did wrong. In his pitiful state he recognized his own faults and began the process of repentance.

As he truly set his heart toward the Lord his strength returned to him. His relationship with God was getting restored. His hair was growing back and his vows were being renewed.

Samson had no eyes but he was able to see more clearly than ever before. He saw an opportunity to complete his assignment. He saw victory, he saw the mercies of God.

Then the lords of the Philistines gathered them together for to offer a great sacrifice unto Dagon their god, and to rejoice: for they said, Our god hath delivered Samson our enemy into our hand. And when the people saw him, they praised their god: for they said, Our god hath delivered into our hands our enemy, and the destroyer of our country, which slew many of us. Judges 16:23-24

It was the five lords of the Philistines that thought that their god Dagon delivered Samson into their hands. These are the men who paid Delilah to set him up. They gathered their people together to celebrate their victory and to offer a great sacrifice to Dagon.

They honored this idol but it did not know. They praised it but it could not hear. They celebrated it but it could not see. Dagon was only a useless statue that was carved from stone. He could not walk, nor taste, nor think for himself. He was no god at all. He couldn't hear their cries when they were in the midst of battle much less save them. He could not speak nor give revelation but the Philistines thought this statue, with no life, was able to deliver Samson into their hands. They gathered together to worship it joyfully.

And it came to pass, when their hearts were merry, that they said, Call for Samson, that he may make us sport. And they called for Samson out of the prison house; and he made them sport: and they set him between the pillars. And Samson said unto the lad that held him by the hand, Suffer me that I may feel the pillars whereupon the house standeth, that I may lean upon them. Now the house was full of men and women; and all the lords of the Philistines were there; and there were upon the roof about three thousand men and women, that beheld while Samson made sport. Judges 16:25-27

During the celebration Samson made sport for the Philistines. This means that he entertained them through his humiliation. He was mocked and he was scorned as he stood before the crowd in a wretched state.

They must've said things like, "Where is your God now, Samson? He must've forgotten you. He must no longer care about you."

It is possible that the crowd may have spit on him and treated him in a similar manner that Christ was treated on His way to being crucified.

There are no details to which extent that Samson went through in order to make sport for his enemies. We can only imagine the humiliation he suffered.

This scripture was written to warn us of the possible outcome of a sinful life knowing you were called for so much more. It is also written to instruct those who have found themselves in a similar situation. As long as you have breath, you have hope, and you have an opportunity to surrender to the king.

Samson put himself in this predicament. He made a lot of bad choices during the time of his ministry. He ruined a lot of good opportunities. More than likely he disappointed a lot of people in the process. He was really good at messing things up.

There are many of us who can relate. It is not something that we are proud to admit. It's not like we aim at failure. If we could get things right from the very beginning, we would, but just like Samson we all fall short of God's glory.

How many times have we blown it? Time and time again we fall short. We make mistakes when it comes to marriage, parenting, and leadership. We make mistakes as children of God but this is how we grow. If we do not learn and grow from our mistakes then we will eventually suffer humiliation just as Samson did.

The harder a person falls the harder it is to get back up. Some people fall so hard they never get back up. They stay on the ground becoming spiritually crippled and lame. When we fall we are not supposed to stay down. We have to learn to get back up and walk it out: "For a just *man* falleth seven times, and riseth up again" (Proverbs 24:16).

Samson was a righteous man. We know this because he fell seven times but every time he fell he got back up. A true soldier always gets back up.

And Samson called unto the Lord, and said, O Lord God, remember me, I pray thee, and strengthen me, I pray thee, only this once, O God, that I may be at once avenged of the Philistines for my two eyes. And Samson took hold of the two middle pillars upon which the house stood, and on which it was borne up, of the one with his right hand, and of the other with his left And Samson said, Let me die with the Philistines. And he bowed himself with all his might; and the house fell upon the lords, and upon all the people that were therein. So the dead which he slew at his death were more than they which he slew in his life. Judges 16:28-30

Instead of feeling sorry for himself and allowing misery to dominate his life, Samson prayed. From the depths of his pitiful state he started his prayer with the words, "O Lord God, remember me, I pray thee."

It wasn't because God forgot about him that he prayed this prayer. Samson was asking for a divine remembrance. He wanted God to notice him and acknowledge him as His own. He wanted God to act on his behalf. Every time God remembers someone, He acts on their behalf.

When God remembered Noah, He delivered him from the flood. When God remembered Abraham, He spared his nephew from disaster. When God remembered Racheal, He opened up her womb. When God remembers someone, His involvement becomes evident and you could expect a miracle to take place. Impossibilities become possible to those who are remembered by God. It is no wonder why Samson prayed this prayer.

The writer of Psalm 106 prayed this prayer in verse 4: "remember me oh Lord when you show favor to your people." The thief who was on the cross next to Jesus said, "remember me when you come to your kingdom."

We all want God to remember us when calamity strikes. We want God to act on our behalf in times of need, but it all depends on the condition our heart. This prayer has to go hand in hand with repentance.

God will not acknowledge the prayers of those who regard sin in their hearts. He remembers those who have surrendered their will to Him.

Therefore, we know that Samson's heart was right place during the final moments of his life. He prayed for strength and of course his hair was already growing back. The Holy Spirit was at work in Samson's life once again.

The strength that Samson was asking God to give him was not physical but spiritual. It isn't physical strength that you pray for to move mountains. You ask God to strengthen your faith because faith the size of a mustard seed is what moves mountains. You ask God to strengthen your inner most being because it will reflect on how you perform outwardly. Samson was asking God to strengthen his faith to push down those pillars. It is not by physical strength nor by physical power but by the Spirit of God that we are able to accomplish the impossible. We ask God to increase our faith. We ask Him to strengthen our prayer life so that our relationship with Him will also be strengthened.

We ask Him for strength because we know that we are weak in certain areas. He is the true source of our strength and He provides it through the Holy Spirit.

We have a God given assignment that we must accomplish here on earth. We need the strength of God to accomplish it. Samson was stepping back into his assignment and that is why he prayed for strength.

At this point God was already revealing to Samson what he was supposed to do next. He knew that he would have to do his part to receive a miracle.

After serving God for a period of time you will begin to realize that God moves when you move. You ask God to strengthen you and then you take a step out in faith.

"Strengthen me this once" is translated as "strengthen me one more time." God had given Samson the strength to accomplish the impossible many times before. He wanted God to do it once more. By saying once more he was throwing the history of God's faithfulness up against his present situation.

He said, "Lord, I'm asking you to strengthen me one more time because I have seen you do it before.

I remember what you did for me when the lion attacked me in the vineyard. You showed yourself strong on my behalf so that I was able to tear him to pieces with my bare hands.

I remember how you helped me when my own people tied me up and handed me over to the Philistines. You provided a jawbone and helped me slay a thousand Philistines.

I remember how you helped me when I got surrounded in Gaza at the house of the prostitute. You got me out of that one too Lord. You empowered me to walk away with the city gates.

Lord I need you to strengthen me once more. I need you to help me one more time."

If we ever find ourselves in a similar predicament, where sin has blinded or bound us spiritually, we can always look back to what God has done in past times and say, "Lord, one more time." You have helped me before Lord do it again. You helped me overcome the meth addiction, you helped me overcome the heroin, you helped me out of a toxic relationship. Lord, I need help one more time. Strengthen me once more.

After Samson prayed, he put his hands on the pillars and pushed. Although it doesn't mention any verbal response from God, Samson went ahead and pushed anyway. He pushed with all his might. This is a model example of how we should follow through with our prayers. We all know that true faith produces action. Faith without works is dead.

Therefore after we ask God for help, we must take a step of faith. It's the step that counts. Samson prayed and then he pushed with all his might. He was showing his faith by the work of his hands. He wasn't worried about failure. He wasn't worried about the crowd.

When you ask for help in accomplishing big things you should never be focused on what will happen if you fail. Nor should you worry about what the crowd will think. You can rise above your circumstances even if the crowd is not with you. Just focus on the great things that could happen when you do accomplish what you asked God to help you with.

Keep in mind that God never said it would be easy. He is always willing to provide the strength but we have to put an effort behind it. God strengthened Samson to push down those pillars but Samson did the pushing. In order to finish the race we will have to push with all our might and just like Samson we could finish strong.

From the looks of it, Samson was a master tradesman. He specialized in demolition. He was so good at messing stuff up that God made this a part of his calling. He had been destroying things his whole life but this time he was able to destroy something worth destroying. He destroyed what he was meant to destroy, the house of his enemies.

There are certain things in this life that we are meant to destroy. There is a time to kill. We are meant to destroy everything that the devil has ever built up. If he has a stronghold, we have got to pull it down. This passage refers to the pulling down of strongholds.

In all reality it would have taken some heavy machinery to accomplish what Samson did with his own hands. Demolition is hard labor and many times it requires brainstorming to accomplish the task. The best way to approach these jobs is to think of every alternative outcome.

Samson had to have done some brainstorming in order to figure out that he could accomplish his assignment by pushing down those pillars. He must have also been familiar with the place to know the layout. He knew exactly how this would play out. He thought it through. With the help of the Holy Spirit he came to conclusion that the only way to fulfill his destiny was to die with his enemies. By doing this he would be able to help his people escape their oppression and rebuild his relationship with God at the same time.

This was not a suicide. He was laying his life down for his people. For one to commit suicide is to die in sin. The interpretation of this scripture has nothing to do with suicide. It is not implying that one should take their own life to escape from the shackles of sin. Now if one should lay down their life in a heroic attempt to save others that would be different. That is what Samson did here.

He was listed among the heroes of the faith in Hebrews 11. Although he blew it many times along the way, God still used him. Eventually, Samson got it right and fulfilled his destiny. He did exactly what God called him to do. The prophecy given to Samson's mother by the angel stated that he would begin to deliver Israel out of the hand of the Philistines (Judges 13:5). He wasn't called to completely deliver the people from the hands of the enemy, but that is because God knew exactly how his story would end.

Samson lost his life physically but gained it spiritually. His story was written to give us an idea of what we have to do on a spiritual level. The true interpretation to this scripture teaches us the concept of dying to self: "For whosoever will save his life shall lose it: and whosoever will lose his life for my sake shall find it" (Mathew 16:25). It is the denial of ourselves that leads to the death of our sinful nature. If we truly want to make a difference we have to die to self completely.

Becoming selfless is not a task that any man can do alone. We do it with the power of the Holy Spirit. We crucify the flesh with its passions and desires so that Christ can live through us. According to this scripture, if you die to self you can take your enemies out too. This does not mean you will no longer have opposition but the things that once blinded you and bound you to the point of humiliation will no longer have a grip on you. Dying to self is a daily task. The old selfish man would like to resurrect itself at any given time but we can lean on the strength that God provides. We become stronger as time passes.

Dying to self is the first step to bringing deliverance to God's people. We are not doing this for self only but to help build the kingdom of God. As you begin to surrender full heartedly you will be able to break chains in the life of other people as well: "The Spirit of the Lord GOD is upon me; because the LORD hath anointed me to preach good tidings unto the meek; he hath sent me to bind up the brokenhearted, to proclaim liberty to the captives, and the opening of the prison to them that are bound" (Isaiah 61:1).

Samson was only called to begin the deliverance of his people from the bondage of their enemies. That is exactly what he did. He took the lead but it was David who continued the work. Therefore, take note that we must graduate from a Samson to a David. The Samson in us has to be put to rest in order to reach the next level.

Although you will still make mistakes you will continue the fight and become more effective. From a judge into a king. Yes, you are definitely a king in the making. A king who represents the one and only true King which is Jesus Christ. The King of kings.

In conclusion to this book we find that God uses flawed individuals to accomplish His will. The only perfect person is Jesus Christ. Other than Jesus, God only has the imperfect vessels to use for His glory.

God calls us to make a difference. He wants to use us to change the world but it all starts with the man in the mirror. We have to allow God to work on us in order to be most effective. It is a process and mistakes will happen. Nevertheless as you can see we don't have to let sin keep us from seeking God. God is willing to give chances. As long as we are still alive, we still have a chance to surrender.

He loves us and He wants to use us in spite of all our errors. Our assignments await us and they have not changed.

We are part of God's plan to bring deliverance to His people. We are the hands and feet of our Savior and He wants to use us to lead others to Himself.

Printed in the United States
by Baker & Taylor Publisher Services